ECONOMIC ASSESSMENT OF ELECTION PROGRAMMES

Economic Assessment of Election Programmes

Does it make sense?

Edited by

Johan J. Graafland
Tilburg University,
Tilburg, The Netherlands

and

Arie P. Ros
Erasmus University,
Rotterdam, The Netherlands

KLUWER ACADEMIC PUBLISHERS
BOSTON / DORDRECHT / LONDON

A C.I.P. Catalogue record for this book is available from the Library of Congress.

ISBN 1-4020-7390-9

Published by Kluwer Academic Publishers,
P.O. Box 17, 3300 AA Dordrecht, The Netherlands.

Sold and distributed in North, Central and South America
by Kluwer Academic Publishers,
101 Philip Drive, Norwell, MA 02061, U.S.A.

In all other countries, sold and distributed
by Kluwer Academic Publishers,
P.O. Box 322, 3300 AH Dordrecht, The Netherlands.

Printed on acid-free paper

Printed in the Netherlands.

CONTENTS

CONTRIBUTORS

Eduard J. Bomhoff	Director, NYFER Forum for Economic Research, Breukelen, the Netherlands (until 22 July 2002); Deputy Prime Minister and Minister of Public Health, Welfare and Sport (22 July 2002 – 16 October 2002).
Frank A.G. den Butter	Member of the Scientific Council for Government Policy, The Hague, Fellow of the Tinbergen Institute, and Professor of Economics, Free University of Amsterdam, the Netherlands, Applied Labour Economics Research Team (ALERT), Dept. of Economics.
F.J. Henk Don	Director, CPB Netherlands Bureau for Economic Policy Analysis, The Hague, the Netherlands
Herman H.H. van Erp	Associate professor of Social Philosophy and Ethics, Faculty of Philosophy, Tilburg University, the Netherlands
Leo van der Geest	Research Director, NYFER Forum for Economic Research, Breukelen, the Netherlands
Johan J. Graafland	Professor of Ethics, Politics and Economics, Faculty of Philosophy, Tilburg University, the Netherlands
J.P.A.M. (Jan) Jacobs	Researcher, Macroeconomics Section, Department of Economics, Groningen University, the Netherlands
Hugo A. Keuzenkamp	Managing Director, SEO Amsterdam Economics, and Professor of Applied Economics, Faculty of Economics, University of Amsterdam, the Netherlands
Gerard H. Kuper	Researcher, Macroeconomics Section, Department of Economics, Groningen University, the Netherlands
S.G. (Fieke) van der Lecq	Editor-in-Chief, Economisch Statistische Berichten (ESB), Rotterdam, the Netherlands
Luc van Liedekerke	Associate Professor, European Center for Ethics, Catholic University Leuven (K.U. Leuven), Belgium; Faculty of Philosophy, Tilburg University, the Netherlands

Arie P. Ros Managing Director, Research Center for Economic Policy (OCFEB), Erasmus University of Rotterdam, the Netherlands

Elmer Sterken Professor of Monetary Economics, Department of Economics, Groningen University, the Netherlands

Otto H. Swank Professor of Public Sector Economics, Erasmus University of Rotterdam, the Netherlands, Research Fellow of the Tinbergen Institute and of the Research Center for Economic Policy (OCFEB)

A. (Toon) Vandevelde Professor, Centre of Ethics and Economics, Institute of Philosophy, Catholic University Leuven (K.U. Leuven), Belgium

PREFACE

What do windmills, wooden shoes, tulip bulbs and an independent economic assessment of election programmes have in common? They are all typical Dutch products. As far as we know, the assessment of the election programmes by CPB Netherlands Bureau for Economic Policy Analysis (CPB) on the request of political parties is a unique phenomenon, only carried out on the occasion of the parliamentary elections in the Netherlands. This analysis has preceded every election for national parliament since 1986. Initially, only the three major political parties had their programme examined. Preceding the elections of 15 May 2002, all eight incumbent parties joined in this exercise.

On 19 April 2002, about one month before the elections, we organized a conference on this CPB analysis of election programmes. Economists, philosophers and politicians contributed to this conference, which slightly tongue-in-cheek was titled *Calculated Choices*. This volume contains the papers presented at the conference. Hugo Keuzenkamp, who acted as chairman of the conference, introduces the subject in chapter 1. Chapter 2 provides a summary of the CPB assessment of 2002, written by the institute in charge. Thus the reader who is not familiar with the assessment can get a fair impression of what it is all about. The chapters 3-11 contain the actual papers that were presented at the conference. In chapter 12, Luc van Liedekerke summarizes the views of the political parties involved, as expressed by their representative speakers at the conference. Finally, chapter 13 sums up the main points and draws some conclusions.

Although the assessment of election programmes is unique for the Netherlands, the emphasis of this book is not on the institutional and practical aspects of the matter. The aim is rather to answer more general questions, such as: "Why is this exercise done?", "What is typical for the Dutch policy making process that explains why it is done in the Netherlands and not in other countries?", "What are the pros and cons of such an assessment?", and: "Who benefits from this exercise: the citizens or the political parties?". It is on the other hand inevitable that sometimes only locally known names are used, especially those of Dutch political parties. The pages xi-xii provide some background information.

We would like to thank all contributors to this volume and to the conference. A special word of thanks goes to Henk Don, director of CPB. Without his enthousiastic cooperation the conference would not have been such a success, and this book probably would not have been written. Last but not least we thank Ina Doorn, who did a magnificent job in the organization of the conference as well as in the preparation of this volume.

Johan J. Graafland and Arie P. Ros (Eds.), Economic Assessment of Election Programmes: Does it Make Sense?, ix-x.

Surprising or not, this book is more actual than planned. Already on 16 October 2002, the new Dutch government coalition fell. New elections are settled on 22 January 2003. Most parties will enter the campaign with the same election programme as in the spring of 2002. Thus, the CPB analysis will play again its role in January 2003.

Tilburg/Rotterdam, November 2002

Johan Graafland
Arie Ros

POLITICAL PARTIES IN THE NETHERLANDS

To help the reader who is not familiar with the Dutch political situation, Table 1 gives a bird's-eye view of the parties involved. It provides some key information on the Dutch political parties represented in national parliament. The first two columns give their full names in Dutch as well as the acronyms commonly used. Since some of the names will certainly not ring a bell to many foreign readers, the third column gives a literal translation in English. Unfortunately, even then it might not be immediately clear what the party in question stands for. Therefore, in the column "profile" we have tried to characterize the parties as concise and as fair as we can. This is of course a delicate job to do, but we have relied as much as possible on the information of the party websites themselves. The next column provides the web addresses, so that verification (or a quest for more information) is quickly possible.

The last three columns present the seats in parliament, for the period 1998-2002, for the situation after the elections of 15 May 2002, as well as for the imaginary election result at the end of October 2002, according to the polls of that moment. Comparing these columns, it immediately becomes clear that the 2002 elections brought about a political landslide. Entering the elections with a comfortable majority of 97 of the 150 seats in parliament, the so-called "purple coalition" of PvdA, VVD and D66 at the end of the day found itself almost halved. The loss was quite evenly distributed over the three parties. Out of the blue came the new party LPF with an unprecedented gain of 26 seats. Moreover, CDA, having been out of office for eight years, increased with almost fifty per cent. The message of the voters was clear: "old" politics were out, "new" politics were in. This was especially true for the LPF, having the battle against the political establishment as its main item. To what extent the murder of its leader Pim Fortuyn on 6 May 2002 (just ten days before the elections) influenced the election results, will probably always remain unknown. However, the most recent polls show that the life span of the new parties is probably very short. The "old" parties seem to be collecting the votes of the "new" parties.

With respect to the theme of this book, it is interesting to observe that the newcomers in parliament, the above mentioned LPF and the small LN, refused to join the assessment exercise. Whether or not this implies a reversal of the trend towards joining the exercise more and more, is at present unclear. These two parties anyhow proved that it is still possible to compete successfully in the elections without having one's election programme examined by CPB.

Johan J. Graafland and Arie P. Ros (Eds.), Economic Assessment of Election Programmes: Does it Make Sense?, xi-xii.

Table 1. Dutch political parties in a nutshell

Name	Acronym	Name in English	Profile	Website	Seats 1998-2002	Seats after 15 May 2002	Poll week 43, 2002
Partij van de Arbeid*	PvdA*	Labour Party	Social Democrat	www.pvda.nl	45	23	31
Volkspartij voor Vrijheid en Democratie*‡	VVD*‡	People's Party for Freedom and Democracy	(Conservative) Liberal	www.vvd.nl	38	24	29
Christen Democratisch Appèl‡	CDA‡	Christian Democratic Appeal	Christian Democrat	www.stemcda.nl	29	43	51
Democraten 66*	D66*	Democrats 66	Social (Progressive) Liberal	www.D66.nl	14	7	6
GroenLinks	GL	Green Left	Progressive Environmentalist	www.groenlinks.nl	11	10	11
Socialistische Partij	SP	Socialist Party	(Left wing) Socialist	www.sp.nl	5	9	14
ChristenUnie	CU	Christian Union	Orthodox Protestant	www.christenunie.nl	5	4	3
Staatkundig Gereformeerde Partij	SGP	Reformed Political Party	Orthodox Protestant	www.sgp.nl	3	2	3
Lijst Pim Fortuyn‡	LPF‡	List Pim Fortuyn	Anti Political Establishment, main items: ▪ public order and safety, ▪ immigration, ▪ public health	www.lijstpimfortuyn.nl	-	26	2
Leefbaar Nederland	LN	Livable Netherlands	Anti Political Establishment, main items: as LPF, but somewhat less conservative	www.leefbaar.nl	-	2	0

*Member of the coalition, 1988-2002.
‡Member of the coalition, 2002-2002.

PART 1

INTRODUCTION

CHAPTER 1

HUGO A. KEUZENKAMP

A DAY OF RECKONING FOR POLITICIANS – OR ECONOMISTS?

1. FROM TINBERGEN'S LEGACY TO DUTCH FOLKLORE

Jan Tinbergen is one of the fathers of quantitative policy analysis based on economic models. Nowhere is his legacy more cherished than in the Netherlands, where up till today, CPB Netherlands Bureau for Economic Policy Analysis (CPB) (which he helped to found) plays an authoritative role as the government advisory agency for economic policy preparation.[1]

Tinbergen regarded economic policy as a technical optimum problem: given political preferences on economic goals (growth, income distribution, *et cetera*), and given the structure of the economy, the question is how different instruments should be used to realise some policy goals.[2] Political preferences could be captured in a social welfare function, and the structure of the economy was reflected in an econometric model. The economist should advise which instruments would serve the purpose.

Can the use of models be extended, from policy makers to the voters who elect them? CPB and Dutch political parties seem to think so. In 1986, the three largest political parties asked CPB to review their election programmes. The Netherlands suffered more than other countries from the economic crisis: corporate defaults, rising unemployment, exploding budget deficits and high inflation defined the election battleground. Politicians sought credibility for their alternative views, CPB was asked to judge the economic proposals. Ever since the 1986 election, CPB analysed election programmes, where an increasing number of political parties signed up for the exercise. CPB calculates the likely effects of respective programmes on employment, budget deficits, income distribution and other relevant economic variables.

Johan J. Graafland and Arie P. Ros (Eds.), Economic Assessment of Election Programmes: Does it Make Sense?, 3-6.

The results are usually front page news of the national newspapers, even though they are rarely shocking. The direct impact on voting behaviour is probably small, with perhaps one minor exception (when the Christian Democrats CDA did not score as good as they had expected in the calculations). Still, the exercise is considered to be important as well as controversial. It certainly has become part of Dutch economic folklore – the exercise is unique in the world.

2. CONTROVERSY

Proponents of the audit regard it as a useful disciplining device, that encourages political parties to make their promises realistic and consistent. Policy proposals have to be made "operational" – cheap talk will not be processed by CPB. It is thought to be a service to the public, by showing voters how and to what degree political parties are able to realise their preferences. It also levels the playing field on economic arguments. All parties accept the baseline projections of CPB and accept the same definitions for employment, budget *et cetera*. Debates can be more substantive, when the real differences are on policies rather than quibbling about the background numbers. This also helps in the phase after the elections, when coalition formation is at stake. Again, the general economic background does not have to be a matter of argument, and operational proposals can be discussed.

At the same time, criticism of the exercise has always been strong. Some critics doubt whether a government agency should be allowed to judge election programs. In their view, it is the world upside down, when civil servants examine political parties. Others doubt whether CPB is up to this task. The models and economic interpretations of CPB are not sacrosanct. Perhaps the models may be suitable for the analysis of marginal policy changes, but not for drastic structural changes proposed by some parties. Crucial economic variables may be missing, relations may be mis-specified. In the worst case, political parties will propose policies that are rewarded by a stamp of approval from CPB, rather than proposing policies that are innovative and promising, but do not fit in the straitjacket of the "official" economic models.

3. THE PRETENCE OF MODELS

Traditionally, CPB has a strong orientation on large structural econometric models for policy analysis. CPB uses a number of such models for the analysis of election programmes (see the contribution of Don in this volume). Are the models good enough for the purpose? And is the additional "expert judgement", that supports the analysis, reliable and accountable?

In academic circles, large structural econometric models have lost much of their popularity. Their predicting quality is weak, certainly compared to more "naïve" time series models, and the interpretation of model output is often very difficult. Additional expert judgement is indispensable, this makes policy analysis based on such use of models nonreplicable.

When experts are authoritative, I would not have great difficulty with the procedure. In many cases, CPB does have authority – *e.g.* in translating world economic conditions to the Dutch economy, or in budget accounting, or infrastructure cost-benefit analysis (although this is disputed by Bomhoff and Van der Geest in this volume). However, major policy shifts in the Netherlands were not always best served by CPB policy analysis. The structural or supply side (rather than Keynesian) effects of tax reduction were not well captured in the models used during the 1980s. Institutional effects of social security reform (high on the agenda around 1990) did not fit in the models. Competition policy and privatization appeared on the CPB research programme long after the first effective steps into that direction were taken. The classic joke of the policeman, who saw an economist at night looking for something by a street lamp, applies. He asked him what he was looking for. The economist said, "I lost my keys somewhere on the other side of the street." The policeman asked him why he was not searching there. The economist responded, "It is a lot easier to look over here."

It may be easier to focus on short term income distribution effects of tax and spending – but as long as the more serious issues are not illuminated, the value added of the exercise is limited.

Still, models can be useful, as long as pretences are kept in control. Many small policy interventions can be analysed with econometric models – although Graafland shows in his contribution that even here, restraint should be taken. He shows that they suffer from serious specification uncertainty. When the confidence margins are taken into account, the differences in outcomes between political programmes become insignificant or occasionally even reverse. Large policy overhauls are more problematic. Ideally, they should lead to a crash of the modelling simulation exercise. Revolutionising the tax system, as GroenLinks proposes, is far beyond the boundaries of the models that are being used. Of course, the models should not have survived the GroenLinks plans. The fact that the calculations did converge is a doubtful accomplishment. Still, CPB publishes results of such an exercise.

Some commentators suggest that different research institutes should be invited to do simultaneous election programme audits (the party leader of GroenLinks hoped to make me happy with such an offer). I do not think this contributes much value. The large scale calculations, especially on government budget and private incomes, need a very serious investment in model infrastructure. CPB does have an appropriate apparatus for this purpose (no complaints here), economies of scale are nearly prohibitive for new entrants. Rather than creating artificial competition, it might be good when CPB makes its toolbox more transparent. Models and the complete databank on the web, and more interaction with academics in order to improve models or inspire a transfer to the museum of outdated instruments.

A related theme is that a number of policy interventions deal with the very way economic policy is set up. Modern politicians endorse the idea of the "learning government", where controlled policy experiments are used to make incremental policy improvements. This methodology is very different from the more traditional CPB approach, where econometric models take the place of experiments. A party that proposes to drop current activating labour policy in favour of yet undefined programmes that are developed on the basis of experiments, will not "score" in the CPB programme analysis. Cheap talk, no operational measures. Perhaps CPB will provide encouraging side comments, but this is not likely to reach the newspapers.

4. WHO BENEFITS: POLITICIANS, VOTERS... OR CPB ITSELF?

Although political parties voluntarily join the analysis, their co-operation may be the result of a prisoners' dilemma. Ad Melkert, former party leader of the Dutch Labour Party (PvdA), once informed me that he would like to make a deal with his colleagues, to stop the political programme analysis of CPB. He was dissatisfied with the false pretences, and with the tendency towards technocratic policy making, where financial specialists of political parties go far beyond the actual election programme in order to put some "flesh" on the bones of the programme. Who controls this process? When the answer would be that a government agency, as CPB is, or a few unaccountable party members are too much in charge, this would harm the democratic political system. Melkert did not want to make his proposal public, as it might be interpreted as weakness. Withdrawal would be interpreted as weakness, even though all parties share some of the criticism.

Still, this does not imply that politicians do not benefit from the CPB analysis. They receive a crash course in economic model analysis. This is useful in itself (politicians deserve better insight in economic principles), and also helps to ease coalition talks after the elections. Whether the evaluation of election programmes is the best way to teach politicians basic economics, may of course be doubted.

It is optimistic to think that voters are served by the CPB exercise. I do not have friends who are deeply impressed by calculations that suggest that a left wing party has slightly better income perspectives for the less well-off, and that a right wing party scores a bit better on long term growth. Such results are not quite unexpected – the surprise may be that differences are so small. Comments by economists in newspapers are probably at least as influential (which still means: not very much), even though many academic economists are, unlike CPB, affiliated to some political party.

Perhaps the highest benefit goes to the economists at CPB. They are forced to deal with serious but at times also eccentric policy ideas, and have to suit their mind and toolbox to processing such ideas. This may stimulate the innovation of model makers, and provides also a useful robustness test for the models that are being used.

NOTES

1 See also Den Butter in this volume.

2 Tinbergen (1956).

REFERENCES:

Tinbergen, J. (1956), *Economic Policy: Principles and Design*, Amsterdam: North-Holland

CHAPTER 2

CPB NETHERLANDS BUREAU FOR ECONOMIC POLICY ANALYSIS

CHARTING CHOICES 2003-2006

Economic Effects of Eight Election Programmes - Summary[*]

1. INTRODUCTION

Election programmes deal with proposed choices. Everyone wants to take measures that cost nothing or have no down sides. But in practice everything has a price tag. For example, a party cannot raise public spending, cut taxes and reduce the public debt all at the same time. With this analysis, CPB Netherlands Bureau for Economic Policy Analysis (CPB) wants to set out the choices which the political parties propose in their election programmes. This will reveal the various preferences they have.

Important elements of the analysis are the summaries of the budgetary, macroeconomic and purchasing power effects of the election programmes. With regard to the budgetary effects, CPB looks at the implications of the proposed measures for income and expenditure of the public sector as a whole, which includes the central government budget in the narrow sense, as well as the budgets for social security and health care. The macroeconomic effects relate to the implications for the Dutch economy: output, employment, consumption, earnings, inflation *et cetera*. Purchasing power effects are not easily expressed in a single figure, because the implications for different types of households vary widely. Hence, in this context dot diagrams and a juxtaposition of the relevant figures for the various groups are presented.

In the course of preparing this study, CPB was also asked by various parties to pay attention to the more qualitative aspects of the proposed policies. In consultation with the parties, a decision was made to conduct an institutional economic analysis of policy intentions in the health care sector. Furthermore, as in 1998 and 1994, the

Johan J. Graafland and Arie P. Ros (Eds.), Economic Assessment of Election Programmes: Does it Make Sense?, 7-20.

parties were able to call on the National Institute of Public Health and the Environment (RIVM) for analyses of the environmental effects of their programmes. The RIVM reported its findings separately.

The VVD and CDA did not commission an analysis of the environmental effects by the RIVM or a qualitative analysis of the health care proposals by CPB. And owing to a lack of resources, the SGP was not able to provide the requested elaboration and explanation of its programme; hence, the CPB analysis of the SGP's programme is limited to an examination of its proposed budgetary policy. This explains why this publication does not present a comprehensive analysis for all eight parties.

The starting point for the analysis is the cautious trend-based scenario for 2003-2006, as published in the Economic Outlook 2003-2006 (CPB, 2001).[1] A week after the publication of the Dutch version of 'Charting Choices' on 27 March 2002 (CPB, 2002a), new projections for 2002 and 2003 were published in the Spring economic forecast 2002 (CPB, 2002c).[2] The new projections do not have any influence on the analysis of the economic effects of the various policy packages. However, the cautious scenario figures will have to be adjusted, with the budget balance amounts in particular coming out differently. These adjustments are the same for all parties, and so they will not distort the mutual comparability of the programmes. Boxes in chapter 3 outline the parties' plans for dealing with a possible deterioration of the budget balance in the reference year 2002. CPB will prepare up-to-date figures for the medium term for use in the coalition negotiations.

The complete publication (in Dutch) is structured as follows. Chapter 1 offers a summary of the main findings. Chapter 2 offers a short description of the economic scenarios, which, without new policies, provide the basis for the analysis of the election programmes. Chapter 3 outlines each party's policy commitments and estimates the budgetary, macroeconomic and purchasing power effects. Chapter 4 focuses on several themes, such as the economic effects of environmental policy, the qualitative analysis of proposals to reform the health care sector, and a more detailed analysis of the proposals related to the Disability Insurance Act ("WAO"). A separate annex sets out each party's specific policy proposals. And finally, two annexes provide supplementary budgetary information and explanations of several economic concepts.

The present text offers a translation of part of the introduction and of the entire first chapter of the complete publication.

2. SUMMARY

The analysis of the economic effects of the election programmes takes as its starting point the cautious scenario without new policies for 2003-2006. CPB outlined this scenario in November 2001.[3] The budgetary calculations are based on the multi-year figures set out in the Budget Memorandum 2002 (Tweede Kamer, 2001-2002), and a projection of health care expenditure without new policies.[4] The scenario is cautious because it allows a safety margin of ¼ percentage point per year in the projection of trend-based economic growth. This margin is clearly smaller than in the cautious scenarios used for the previous two governments' terms of office. Hence, there is a greater chance of setbacks than before, but it is still smaller than 50%.

Budgetary policy

Table 1 shows the broad outline of the eight parties' budgetary policy proposals. All parties call for additional spending on education, health care and public safety. In the baseline scenario without new policies, spending in these policy areas already increases by 7 billion euro (in 2002 prices) in 2003-2006. On top of this figure the parties make further commitments ranging from around 2½ billion euro (VVD, D66, ChristenUnie) to 3½ billion euro (PvdA, CDA, GroenLinks and SGP) and more than 6 billion euro (SP). The additional resources are earmarked for a range of policy measures, including wage increases in the education system, a reduction of waiting lists in the health care sector, and raising the number of police officers on the beat.

GroenLinks and the SP opt for significant cuts in defence spending (0.9 billion euro and 2.9 billion euro respectively). The other parties plan either modest cuts (PvdA, D66), some additional spending (VVD, CDA and ChristenUnie), or no change (SGP) compared to the 0.3 billion euro growth in real terms in the baseline scenario.

Table 1 Expenditure policy in broad outline, 2003-2006

	PvdA	*VVD*	*CDA*	*D66*	*GL*	*CU*	*SP*	*SGP*
	billion euro, 2002 prices							
Balance of additional spending (+) and cutbacks (-)								
Education, health care and public safety	3.3	2.3	3.4	2.5	3.4	2.2	6.2	3.3
Defence and public administration	-2.3	-2.3	-2.1	-1.4	-2.4	-0.9	-2.9	-0.8
Infrastructure and environment	0.6	0.9	1.0	1.4	0.3	1.1	0.8	0.6
Social security and development aid	-0.2	-2.2	-1.0	-0.6	1.6	0.6	3.2	0.6
Other	-0.4	-0.7	-1.3	0.0	-0.3	-0.2	0.8	-0.7
Total net expenditure	1.0	-2.1	0.1	2.0	2.6	2.8	8.1	3.0

With the exception of the SP, all parties propose savings in public administration, ranging from 1.1 billion euro (D66, ChristenUnie) to 2.5 billion euro (VVD). Often these are in the form of normative budget cuts at central government level, and sometimes in the form of restrictions on funding for municipalities and provinces. These savings reduce the increase in spending on public administration amounting to 2.7 billion euro in real terms in the baseline scenario. Four parties (VVD, CDA, D66 and SGP) want to save on balance on jobs created under the Inflow and Throughflow ("I/D") scheme and under the Employment of Job Seekers Act ("WIW") and Sheltered Employment Act ("WSW"). In contrast, the ChristenUnie and the SP advocate modest additional spending. The PvdA and GroenLinks opt for unchanged policies here. Through changes in asylum policy the VVD and CDA save 0.3 billion euro. In contrast, GroenLinks's asylum policy will lead to additional spending of 0.2 billion euro. The SP reserves 0.1 billion euro to improve support for asylum seekers. The other parties' proposed asylum policies have no budgetary effects.

All parties earmark additional funds for infrastructure and/or the environment. With the PvdA, VVD, CDA, ChristenUnie and SGP the emphasis is on infrastructure, with GroenLinks and the SP on the environment. All parties earmark additional funds for public transport infrastructure. During the next government's term of office, D66, GroenLinks, the ChristenUnie and SP want to introduce road pricing as a means of reducing traffic congestion.

The largest differences among the parties in budgetary policy are to be found in social security and development aid. The VVD reduces the real growth in development aid that is included in the baseline scenario to zero, while GroenLinks, the ChristenUnie and SP all argue for an increase of 1.0 billion euro. In social security the commitments range from 1.8 billion euro cutbacks by the VVD to 2.2 billion euro additional spending by the SP. Most of the savings in the social security sphere relate to the Disability Insurance Act ("WAO"). Section 4.3 (in the Dutch publication) gives an overview of the parties' WAO proposals. Other proposals include the reintroduction of the obligation to seek work for unemployed people over the age of 57½ years (VVD, CDA, D66, ChristenUnie), the decentralization of welfare benefit financing (VVD, CDA, D66, ChristenUnie) and additional benefit increases (CDA: basic state pension; GroenLinks and SP: all benefits).

Finally, the parties identify larger or smaller savings in other policy areas, in particular by reducing subsidies and/or increasing non-tax revenues (such as fines). Only the SP plans higher spending of 0.8 billion euro through net increases in various subsidies. With the exception of D66 and the SGP, all parties specifically reduce subsidies for businesses, on exports and technology for instance. The CDA and D66 propose significant subsidy cuts across the board. Four parties (PvdA, VVD, CDA and GroenLinks) want to impose a levy or reduce subsidies to stimulate a more active use of the large equity held by housing corporations for urban renewal projects. The VVD and SGP save on the government's contribution to the broadcasting services. With the exception of the SGP, all parties call for an increase in the national budget for culture. The ChristenUnie and SP use the additional allocation to reduce museum admission prices.

Without new policies, total net public spending in the cautious scenario for 2003-2006 will increase by an average of 1¾% per year in real terms (cumulatively by 12¾ billion euro). Because of the cuts and increases proposed by the various parties, this growth figure changes (see Table 2).[5] Including new policies, the additional spending in real terms ranges from 1½% per year (VVD) to 2¾% per year (SP). Table 2 also shows how the eight parties' commitments affect the levels of real growth in the various spending clusters. The growth figures for education and health care are at least 3% per year in real terms. All the parties' commitments on public administration at national level result in low growth, and in some cases even fractionally negative growth.

Table 2 Real growth in net public spending, cautious scenario 2003-2006, including party policies[a]

	PvdA	*VVD*	*CDA*	*D66*	*GL*	*CU*	*SP*	*SGP*
	% per year							
Education	4	3½	4	4¼	4¼	3	5¼	4
Health care	4	3½	4¼	3½	4¼	4	5½	4
Public safety	4¼	4¼	4¼	3½	2¾	3½	3	4¾
Defence	1	1¾	1¾	1	-1½	1¾	-12¾	1¼
Municipalities and Provinces	1	1	1¼	2½	0	2¼	2½	2½
Other public administration	0	-¼	0	¼	¾	¼	1	½
Infrastructure	1¾	3	2¾	2	-1	2½	¾	1½
Social security[b]	2½	1½	2	2¼	2¾	2¼	3½	2½
Development aid	2	0	2	2	6½	6½	6½	4¼
Total net expenditure[c]	1¾	1½	1¾	2	2	2	2¾	2

[a] Excluding macroeconomic effects of the programmes.
[b] Including student grants and contributions towards education and school costs.
[c] Excluding loans and sale of state-owned assets, including other spending such as on the environment.

On the revenue side, nearly all parties opt for higher taxes and levies on polluting activities and for burden relief on labour. With regard to taxes on capital and profits and other taxes (including excise duties on tobacco and alcohol), most parties opt for cuts on balance, but some for increases. Moreover, the measures affecting the various components vary widely (see Table 3). All in all, the VVD, CDA, D66 and PvdA opt, to a greater or lesser extent, for net burden relief, GroenLinks for a neutral stance, and the SP, SGP and ChristenUnie for a net increase.

Table 3 Revenue policy in broad outline, 2003-2006

	PvdA	*VVD*	*CDA*	*D66*	*GL*	*CU*	*SP*	*SGP*
	billion euro, 2002 prices							
Net tax increases (+) and cuts (-)								
Environment	3.5	0.2	0.0	1.7	14.6	3.6	2.6	0.4
Earned income and benefits	-2.4	-1.1	-1.9	-2.3	-18.3	-2.1	-1.0	0.2
Capital and profits	-1.4	-2.3	-0.1	-0.1	3.3	-0.7	3.5	0.5
Other	0.0	0.0	0.0	-0.1	0.4	0.7	0.1	0.8
Total tax and social security contributions	-0.4	-3.2	-2.0	-0.8	0.0	1.5	5.2	1.8

In the cautious scenario the budgetary scope was estimated at 3½ billion euro. This broadly means that without new policies, government revenues will increase by 3½ billion euro more in real terms than public spending. Table 4 shows how much parties want to extend this scope through spending cuts and in some cases also through net tax increases. Including the budgetary effects of the longer-term macroeconomic impact yields the total scope, which is then allocated between additional spending commitments, net burden relief and improving the budget balance. For every ½ billion euro improvement in the budget balance, the budget surplus (*i.e.* the EMU balance) will come out 0.1 percentage point of GDP higher in 2006 than in 2002. In the cautious scenario of November 2001, the EMU balance in 2002 comes out at 0.6% of GDP.

Table 4 Structure and allocation of the budgetary scope, 2003-2006

	PvdA	*VVD*	*CDA*	*D66*	*GL*	*CU*	*SP*	*SGP*
	billion euro, 2002 prices							
Scope in cautious scenario	3½	3½	3½	3½	3½	3½	3½	3½
Spending cuts	3¼	6	6¼	4¾	6	3¾	5¼	2½
Net tax increases						1½	5¼	1¾
Beneficial budgetary effects	0	0	¾	-½	-1¼	-¼	¼	n.a.
Total scope	6¾	9½	10¼	7¾	8¼	8½	14	7¾
Allocated towards:								
additional spending	4¼	3¾	6¼	6½	8½	6½	13¼	5½
net burden relief	½	3¼	2	¾				
improved budget balance	2¼	2½	2¼	¼	-½	1¾	¾	2¼

The macroeconomic impact of the policy packages has no major budgetary consequences for most parties. Most additional spending commitments and most forms of burden relief do produce positive knock-on effects,[6] especially through a broadening of the tax base and a reduction in the unemployment benefit volume. Against this there are the mirror-image negative knock-on effects of most spending cuts and tax increases. On balance, the net knock-on effects are small compared to those found in the programme analysis in 1998. This is due in part to the different economic conditions in the baseline scenario and in part to the greater weight of programme elements with small positive, or large negative knock-on effects for the government budget (see box).

Macroeconomic effects

Table 5 shows the results of the macroeconomic analysis on the basis of a number of selected indicators. The results for the four largest parties (in terms of seats in Parliament before the 2002 elections) are discussed first, then those for the four smaller parties.[7] The estimated effects of the policy packages are additional to the figures for the cautious scenario without new policies, which are shown in the first column. Less value should be attached to the precise level of the scenario figures than to the different effects of the election programmes.[8] The three largest parties are able to nudge GDP growth slightly higher than the 2½% of the cautious scenario without new policies. However, there is a striking difference in potential growth: the VVD package pushes the annual rate of potential growth 0.5 percentage points higher than the 2¼% of the cautious baseline scenario. The effect of the PvdA package on potential GDP, at 0.1 percentage point per year, is the same as the normal GDP effect. And the CDA package holds an intermediate position between these two (0.2 percentage points). The reason for these differences in potential growth must be sought above all in the policy differences on burden relief and social security spending (especially disability benefits): the wedge, the replacement rate[9] and the eligibility for disability benefits are major determinants of the effectively available labour supply. The downside of high potential growth in the VVD package is relatively low household income growth in the short term: the supply-oriented policies carry a price tag in terms of modest real wage increases and a lower replacement rate. To a lesser extent the same applies to the CDA package. As a result, private consumption also grows less in the VVD and CDA packages than in those of the other parties.

Because the three largest parties all end up with a budget surplus (EMU balance) of 1.0% of GDP in 2006, this is not a source of differences as to what is feasible in other areas during the government's term of office. But because of the difference in potential growth, there are differences in the prospects after 2006: the structural budget surplus is clearly higher in the VVD programme, while the CDA programme also has a positive effect on the EMU balance after 2006.

The programmes of the PvdA, VVD and CDA push up annual employment growth from ¾% per year in the cautious scenario without new policies to 1% per year, a policy effect of 0.2-0.3 percentage points per year. However, the composition of employment growth differs sharply between the three parties. With the PvdA the emphasis is on employment in the public sector, where growth in full-time equivalents (fte's) is raised from 1¼% per year to 1½% per year. On balance, the CDA aims for the same rate of employment growth in the public sector as in the baseline scenario, and its positive employment effects are achieved entirely in the market sector. In the VVD's programme employment growth in the public sector is limited to barely 1% per year, while employment growth in the market sector climbs to more than 1% per year.

Why are the positive knock-on effects so much smaller than in 1998?

In 1998, CPB analysed the economic effects of the election programmes of the PvdA, CDA, VVD, D66 and GroenLinks.[a] The positive knock-on effects of the programmes which the same parties have submitted this time, are around 2 billion euro smaller in four cases; only for the CDA do the positive knock-on effects come out slightly higher than in 1998.
There are, of course, many differences between now and then, both in terms of the programmes' contents and in the nature of the economic conditions which the parties face.[b] The following factors account to a large extent for the difference in the knock-on effects:

In contrast with four years ago, the baseline scenario is now characterised by a tight labour market. This makes it more difficult to achieve favourable employment effects, and it also means that on average the positive knock-on effects of burden relief and spending increases are smaller.

Cutbacks with relatively large adverse budgetary effects this time have a greater weight in the election programmes than in 1998. For instance, in the case of measures to reduce the number of disability benefit ("WAO") recipients, the smaller WAO volume (*ex ante* savings) is offset in the first instance by a higher volume of unemployment benefit recipients (negative knock-on effect). In 1998 the four largest parties also planned various amounts of lower contributions to the European Union, a saving which has no negative knock-on effects for the Dutch economy.

Additional spending commitments with relatively small positive knock-on effects this time have a greater weight in the election programmes than in 1998. Thus, four years ago various spending increases were deliberately conceived in labour-intensive terms in order to reduce unemployment.

A number of parties are opting for tax increases with relatively large negative knock-on effects. For instance, environmental levies may achieve the intended behavioural changes which at the same time erode the budgetary gains.

[a] CPB (1998).

[b] There are also differences in the analytical instruments used. These are largely related to the need to set out the economic relationships in a tight labour market situation.

Table 5 Macroeconomic effects, 2003-2006

	baseline scenario	*PvdA*	*VVD*	*CDA*	*D66*	*GL*	*CU*	*SP*
	% per year	*effect on annual growth in percentage points*						
Economic growth								
GDP	2½	0.1	0.1	0.1	0.0	-0.2	0.1	0.0
GDP, potential	2¼	0.1	0.5	0.2	0.1	-0.2	0.0	-0.1
Private consumption	3	0.1	-0.2	-0.1	0.1	0.1	0.0	0.0
Public spending[a]	1½	0.2	-0.1	0.1	0.0	0.0	0.3	0.0
Labour productivity, market sector	2¼	0.0	-0.2	-0.1	0.0	-0.4	0.0	0.0
Wages and prices								
Contractual wages	3½	0.1	-1.1	-0.5	-0.3	-0.6	-0.1	-0.2
Consumer price index	1¾	0.2	-0.4	-0.1	0.2	0.6	0.3	0.2
Real labour costs, market sector	2	0.1	-0.7	-0.3	-0.1	-1.0	-0.1	0.0
Labour market								
Employment (fte)	¾	0.2	0.3	0.2	0.1	0.3	0.2	0.2
Employment, market sector (fte)	¾	0.0	0.4	0.2	0.1	0.1	0.1	0.0
Employment, public sector (fte)	1¼	0.3	-0.3	0.0	-0.4	0.5	0.3	0.2
	level 2006	*effect on level in 2006 in percentage points*						
Unemployment (in %)	4¾	-0.3	-0.2	-0.3	0.2	-0.3	-0.2	-0.2
Equilibrium unemployment (in %)	4¾	-0.2	-0.8	-0.5	-0.1	-0.3	-0.1	0.3
Various								
Replacement rate (in %)	71	0.1	-4.7	-2.5	-0,6	-1.3	-1.4	0.9
Profitability indicator[b] (in %)	8¼	0.0	1.7	0.6	0.2	0.3	0.2	-0.1
		level 2006, including policies						
EMU balance (in % GDP)		1.0	1.0	1.0	0.6	0.5	0.9	0.7
EMU balance, structural (in % GDP)		0.9	2.0	1.4	0.9	0.6	0.8	0.4

[a] Public spending broadly corresponds to government expenditure excluding social security, development aid, subsidies and interest payment.

[b] The profitability indicator is defined as the capital share of enterprise income in the market sector, net of corporation taxes.

The positive employment effects mean that with the three largest parties employment comes out 0.8-1% higher cumulatively by 2006, compared to the baseline scenario. The projected unemployment percentage for 2006 comes out slightly lower with the PvdA than with the VVD, but the VVD's programme clearly offers a better outcome in terms of the equilibrium unemployment level. The VVD's policies are likely to lead to a considerable further fall in unemployment after 2006, in line with the high growth in potential GDP. Under the PvdA's policies, unemployment will nudge upwards after 2006, because pay rates and labour demand in the market sector will not yet have been fully matched to the supply. With the CDA the effect on unemployment in 2006 is the same as with the PvdA, and a further fall is likely after 2006, although it will not be as sharp as with the VVD. Equilibrium unemployment comes out at around 4¼% with the CDA, compared to 4% with the VVD and 4½% with the PvdA.

The PvdA's policy package has a small upward effect on inflation, owing to some upward wage pressure and higher environmental levies. Unlike the PvdA, the VVD and CDA opt for a lower replacement rate and a substantial package of burden relief, so that they are able to achieve a moderation in contractual pay rates in two ways. Consequently business profitability develops relatively favourably with the VVD and CDA, and inflation may also come out lower. The modest increase in real labour costs stimulates employment in the market sector, but will also be accompanied by relatively low growth in labour productivity. The scale of the VVD's plans in this sphere is clearly greater than the CDA's.

The four smaller parties stress different aspects in different ways. D66 combines a relatively good environmental result (see section 4.1 in the Dutch publication) with a positive effect on potential GDP. D66's decision to reduce the number of subsidized jobs depresses employment growth in the public sector. The labour supply is expanded by measures in the social security sphere and the tax system. Against the pay-moderating effects of the additional labour supply, there are upward effects on labour costs owing to the abolition of the targeted reduction of social insurance contributions ("SPAK") and the extension of pension rights. On balance the downward effect on real labour costs is limited until 2006, so that the market sector shows hardly any additional employment growth. The proposed tax measures stimulate part-time working, so that employment growth in persons comes out 0.1 percentage point higher than in the baseline scenario. Unemployment in 2006 comes out slightly higher than in the baseline scenario, but after 2006 it will fall to an equilibrium level that is actually slightly lower than in the baseline scenario without new policies. Because the adjustment process to a structural equilibrium will not have been completed by 2006 in the D66 package, the budget surplus in 2006 will not yet have reached its structural level of 0.9% of GDP.

GroenLinks has an ambitious environmental programme, with high levies on polluting activities. This not only leads to relatively high inflation, in some sectors it also erodes competitiveness to such an extent that domestic production activity in those sectors will fall sharply. Both the actual and potential GDP growth will therefore come out significantly lower than in the baseline scenario without new policies. Despite these negative effects, the high environmental levies generate substantial revenues, which are used by GroenLinks for targeted burden relief on labour. For this reason real labour costs can develop relatively favourably, and employment growth in the market sector is not compromised. In the public sector GroenLinks aims for relatively high employment growth. The consequence of this is that the budget balance does not improve in the next government's term of office.

The ChristenUnie puts a strong emphasis on government spending. But because investments, expenditure on goods and services, the level of government wages and subsidies account for a relatively large share of the additional commitments, the effect on employment growth in the public sector is less pronounced. The spending impulse stimulates GDP growth during the next government's term of office, and indirectly also employment growth in the market sector. Against the tax increases in the ChristenUnie package, there is a fall in the replacement rate, so that real labour costs are barely affected on balance. Unemployment in 2006 comes out lower than in the baseline scenario, but only part of this gain is of a structural nature. The budget balance improves to 0.9% of GDP in 2006, while the structural figure is fractionally lower.

The SP, finally, opts for higher benefits and robust environmental policies. The higher replacement rates and the considerable tax increases lead to a higher structural level of unemployment, with equilibrium unemployment climbing to more than 5%. The redistribution of income brings a spending impulse over the short term, so that GDP growth is not compromised during the next government's term of office. However, potential growth comes out slightly lower, so that the structural budget balance also comes out on the low side. Against this there are benefits in the environmental sphere.

Purchasing power

The election programmes influence purchasing power in many ways, such as through changes in the tax system, measures in the sphere of social security and reforms in health care provision financing. The indirect effect of these measures on wages and prices is also important for purchasing power. Table 6 shows purchasing power changes in the cautious scenario, including the effects of the election programmes. The purchasing power figures take account of different forms of income, such as income from employment, benefits, subsidies, pensions and capital. The figures relate solely to households of employees, civil servants, benefit recipients and pensioners. The purchasing power of most households increases, but not always to the same degree: the income distribution also changes. The average purchasing power increases and the redistribution effects differ from party to party. To illustrate these effects, Table 6 shows the median[10] purchasing power changes for a number of different household groups. The differentiation is provided in four dimensions: income level, labour market situation, age, and household situation.

Low-income households, that is to say, those with incomes below the compulsory health insurance limit, will fare better in relative terms than high-income households with the CDA, GroenLinks, ChristenUnie and SP. These parties' programmes thus provide for a certain levelling of incomes. With the PvdA and D66 the purchasing power increase for low- and high-income households is the same. The VVD's policies lead to a widening of income differentials: the purchasing power of low-income households increases by only ½% per year, while high-income households will on average be 1¼% per year better off.

Benefit recipients fare better in purchasing power terms than employees with the CDA, ChristenUnie, GroenLinks and SP. The gap is widest with the SP, where the purchasing power of benefit recipients increases by an average of 3% per year and that of employees by 1¼% per year. The opposite applies with the VVD and D66, while there is no difference between the two groups with the PvdA. With the VVD the gap is relatively wide: benefit recipients will on average be ¼% per year worse off[11], while employees see their purchasing power increase by 1¼% per year.

With most parties, there is little difference between purchasing power changes for households where the main earner is older than 65 years, and for other households. An exception is GroenLinks, where older people's purchasing power increases by 1%, while other households will be 2¼% better off. This is a consequence of GroenLinks's plans to integrate premiums for the state pension benefit ("AOW") into the tax system, which means that older people with a supplementary pension will pay more tax. With the VVD, the increase in older people's purchasing power also lags somewhat behind that of other households. With the ChristenUnie and the SP the effect on older people's purchasing power is slightly greater than that for other households.

The difference in purchasing power trends by household situation are relatively small in the programmes of the PvdA, D66 and ChristenUnie. With the VVD the purchasing power of multi-person households increases relatively more than that of single-person households. The programmes of the CDA and SP work out relatively well for single-income households and single-person households compared to double-income households. With GroenLinks double-income and single-person households fare better than single-income households. This is due to the restriction of the tax credit for non-working partners.

Table 6 Purchasing power effects 2003-2006, cautious scenario including party policies

	PvdA	*VVD*	*CDA*	*D66*	*GL*	*CU*	*SP*
	median purchasing power changes in % per year						
Low income[a]	1½	½	1½	1	2¼	1¼	2½
High income[a]	1½	1¼	1	1	1½	1	1
Benefit recipient[b]	1½	-¼[d]	1½	¾	2¾	1¼	3
Employee	1½	1¼	1¼	1	2	1	1¼
65 years and older[c]	1½	½	1¼	¾	1	1¼	2
Younger than 65	1½	1¼	1¼	1	2¼	1	1½
Single-income	1¾	1½	1½	1	¾	1¼	2
Double-income	1½	1¼	1	1	1¾	1	1½
Single persons	1½	¾	1½	¾	2	1¼	2

[a] Low incomes are households with an income below the compulsory health insurance limit (30,700 euro for those aged younger than 65 years and 19,550 euro for those aged 65 and older); high incomes are all other households.
[b] Excluding households which receive a basic state pension benefit ("AOW").
[c] Households where the main earner receives an AOW-benefit (possibly with a supplementary pension).
[d] The VVD intends to correct this loss of purchasing power, see footnote 11 in the text.

As mentioned, Table 6 shows median purchasing power changes. That is to say, within each group half of all households will be better off than the figure shown and half will be worse off. This does not take account of the fact that specific groups of households experience a considerably less favourable change in purchasing power. This is true in particular for high-income and affluent households in the programmes of GroenLinks and the SP, for they will face substantial tax increases. The skewed distribution of purchasing power changes is evident from the dot diagrams in chapter 3 in the Dutch version. Another important factor is that the self-employed and company directors are not included in the purchasing power figures; these are often also households with relatively high incomes and assets, which will experience less favourable purchasing power effects with GroenLinks and the SP.

Conclusion

Among the wider public, the CPB analysis is invariably described as a 'calculation' of the election programmes. The public's interest in the analysis focuses on how the quantitative results for the various parties compare, and often for only a few variables. The outcomes are then almost treated – without justification – as performance scores.

However, the purpose of this report is to illustrate the choices which the various parties are making. A good result on one variable invariably means a lower score on another one. Sometimes the dilemmas are contained within the financial and economic sphere, but sometimes the downside of the results will be evident in another sphere, such as the environment or the quality of the education system. This summary offers an insight into the financial and economic policy choices made by the parties involved. This can then be used as a starting point for public debate and as an information source for the voter.

NOTES

* This chapter has been previously published in a more comprehensive version (CPB, 2002b). That publication also addresses the history of the assessment of election programmes, its usefulness and limitations, and the possibility of misuse. In chapter 3 of this volume, Henk Don already goes into these questions more deeply. To avoid unnecessary overlap, these passages have therefore been omitted from the present chapter. The text has been reproduced with permission of CPB Netherlands Bureau for Economic Policy Analysis.

1 An English summary of this report is presented in Huizinga (2001).

2 An English summary of the projections of the Central Economic Plan 2002 is presented in CPB (2002d).

3 CPB (2001). An English summary of this Economic Outlook 2003-2006 was published in Huizinga (2001).

4 Folmer *et al.* (2001) (only in Dutch).

5 In addition there is the longer-term macroeconomic impact of the programmes, especially on the unemployment benefit volume and interest payments. These effects have not been included in Table 2, but they have in Table 4 and beyond.

6 Positive and negative knock-on effects represent the changes in the EMU balance caused by the macroeconomic carry-over of the proposed policy measures. A positive knock-on effect is an improvement of the EMU balance, a negative knock-on effect a deterioration of the EMU balance. An example may clarify this: suppose that a political party intends to increase government consumption by 1 billion euro. This will initially reduce the EMU balance (*ex ante*) by 1 billion euro. Because of this measure government consumption and production will increase, which will increase employment and reduce unemployment. The tighter labour market will result in higher wages. The EMU balance will improve because of less unemployment benefits: a positive knock-on effect. The

EMU balance will further improve, because higher wages and employment will result in higher tax revenues on wages and higher VAT-revenues. The higher wage rate also leads to a negative knock-on effect, because government wages will rise. On balance, a positive knock-on effect will result: the increase in government consumption reduces the EMU balance, including macroeconomic carry-over (*ex post*), by less than 1 billion euro.

7 No macroeconomic analysis was carried out for the SGP programme, because the party did not have the resources to provide the necessary supplementary information.

8 This is why, as usual, the figures for the baseline scenario have been rounded to quarters of a percent and the policy effects to tenths of a percent.

9 The replacement rate measures the ratio between the net income out of work and that in work.

10 The median purchasing power increase means that half of the household group in question experiences a higher purchasing power increase and half a lower increase.

11 A small proportion of the burden-relief measures do not have the effect intended by the VVD, so that benefit recipients come out at –¼ % in Table 6. Part of the tax credit which VVD applies is not payable, because it exceeds the income tax and social security contribution liability. In the time available it was not possible to correct this problem along the lines that the VVD would have wanted, because the budgetary and macroeconomic consequences would have to be recalculated. The VVD is thinking of increasing the special assistance benefit.

REFERENCES

CPB (1998), Charting Choices: Analyzing Five Election Platforms, *CPB Report*, 98/1, 14-18

CPB (2001), *Economische Verkenning 2003-2006* ("Economic Outlook 2003-2006"), The Hague: Sdu Uitgevers

CPB (2002a), *Keuzes in kaart 2003-2006. Economische effecten van acht verkiezingsprogramma's* ("Charting Choices 2003-2006. Economic Effects of Eight Election Programmes"), The Hague: CPB

CPB (2002b), *Charting Choices 2003-2006. Economic Effect of Eight Election Platforms*, CPB Document No. 19, The Hague: CPB

CPB (2002c), *Centraal Economisch Plan 2002* ("Central Economic Plan 2002"), The Hague: Sdu Uitgevers

CPB (2002d), Economic Outlook: The World Economy, the Dutch Economy, and Sectoral Developments in the Dutch Economy, *CPB Report*, 2002/1, 5-20

Folmer, K., E. Mot, R. Douven, E. van Gameren, I. Woittiez, and J. Timmermans (2001), *Een scenario voor de zorguitgaven 2003-2006* ("A Scenario for Health Care Expenditure 2003-2006"), CPB Document No. 007, The Hague: CPB and SCP

Huizinga, F. (2001), Economic Outlook 2003-2006, *CPB Report*, 2001/4, 16-22

Tweede Kamer (2001-2002), *Nota over de toestand van 's Rijks financiën. Miljoenennota 2002* ("Budget Memorandum 2002"), 28 000, nr. 1

CHAPTER 3

F.J. HENK DON

ECONOMIC ANALYSIS OF ELECTION PROGRAMMES: WHAT, HOW AND WHY?

1. INTRODUCTION

On 27 March 2002, CPB Netherlands Bureau for Economic Policy Analysis (CPB) published the report *Keuzes in kaart 2003-2006. Economische effecten van acht verkiezingsprogramma's* ("Charting Choices 2003-2006 - Economic Effects of Eight Election Programmes") (CPB, 2002). This report is the latest specimen of reports by CPB on the economic effects of the election programmes of Dutch political parties. It was published some seven weeks before the general elections for parliament. What is the actual content of the economic analysis performed by CPB on the policy proposals of the election programmes? How does CPB make its assessment of economic effects, what procedure is followed? Why would it be useful, what are the limitations? Why has it become standard practice in the Netherlands and nowhere else? Before tackling these questions, let me briefly sketch the history of the exercise.

In the run-up to the 1986 general elections, the three major political parties (CDA, PvdA, VVD) asked CPB to assess the economic effects of their policy programmes for the next government term (1987-1990). They wanted to have some reassurance as to the feasibility and consistency of their economic policy proposals. The three separate papers prepared by CPB were published jointly after the election (CPB, 1986). In 1989, D66 also requested an analysis. In that year the economic analysis of the four election programmes was published some four weeks before the election (CPB, 1989). In 1994, GroenLinks made the same request as the other parties, so that in that year and in 1998 publications appeared on the economic effects of five election programmes (CPB, 1994 and 1998).

In 2001, all eight political parties present in parliament asked CPB to analyse the economic effects of their election programmes: in addition to the PvdA, VVD, CDA, D66 and GroenLinks, also the CU, the SP, and the SGP. To help them carry out a sound analysis, CPB asked the parties to further elaborate and explain several

Johan J. Graafland and Arie P. Ros (Eds.), Economic Assessment of Election Programmes: Does it Make Sense?, 21-30.

aspects of their programmes. The SGP did not have enough manpower to provide the required explanations and details, so the analysis of its programme was limited to the budgetary effects.

2. WHAT?

What is the actual content of the economic analysis that CPB provides for any particular policy programme? And what is left out?

Contents

The analysis contains three basic elements: the impact on the government budget, the estimated macroeconomic effects, and the effects on the income distribution. The budgetary effects focus on government receipts, expenditures and the budget balance within the government term (four years). They refer to a broad concept of government, which includes not only central government but also the social security system and the health care sector. The macroeconomic analysis estimates the effects for the national economy: on economic growth, employment, private consumption, wages, inflation, *et cetera*. On previous occasions, CPB reported macroeconomic effects four years and eight years into the future. On this occasion CPB gave only effects for the fourth year, but it included estimated effects on structural growth, equilibrium unemployment and the structural budget balance. These three indicate what macroeconomic effects can be expected beyond the next government term.

The effects on the income distribution are not easily captured in a single indicator, because the policy impact on real income tends to differ strongly between various (groups of) households. The 2002 report contains graphical presentations of real income growth for a large sample of private households and provides figures for median real income growth for several groups of households.

In addition to these basic elements, some policy fields may be explored more in depth. Since 1994, the RIVM (National Institute of Public Health and the Environment) has co-operated with CPB to provide an assessment of the environmental effects of the policy programmes. In 1998 the analysis included an assessment of the long-term effects on the labour market of proposed revisions of the tax system. The 2002 report contains an account of the effectiveness of proposed measures for containing the number of disability benefits and a qualitative analysis of proposed changes in the health care system. The latter shows how parties choose between the conflicting targets in designing a health care system: risk solidarity, freedom of choice, incentives for efficiency and efficiency risks.

What is missing?

While the three basic elements of the analysis reveal important economic aspects of the election programmes, many relevant policy targets are excluded. In particular, the analysis does not indicate what the results of the health care policies will be for the health of the population, what education policies will mean for the level of knowledge and training, what the impact of the policy programmes will be on public safety, traffic congestion or the quality of public services. Many of these policy targets are beyond the scope of an economic analysis. More importantly, in most cases we don't know enough about the effects of different policy instruments on the relevant targets. Yet, more could be done, as shown by the joint work of CPB, RIVM, the Spatial Planning Bureau (RPB) and the Social and Cultural Planning Office (SCP) on the merits of a long list of public investment proposals (CPB, RIVM, RPB and SCP, 2002). But a proper assessment would require much more detail in the policy programmes than is already required for the basic analysis. It would also prove to be very costly.

In principle, any effects that proposed policies have on health, level of education, public safety, traffic congestion and the quality of public services, could also affect macroeconomic performance and the government budget. Such indirect effects are absent in the economic analysis. In most cases, such effects are likely to be relatively small and/or only relevant in the longer run, *i.e.* beyond the next government's four year term. This is not to say that these effects are unimportant, but that their impact on the macroeconomic analysis for the four year horizon is likely to be small.

3. HOW?

How does CPB make its assessment of economic effects? What procedure is followed, what instruments are used? What can a political party do to influence the results and what does that mean for their validity?

Baseline

The economic analysis is performed with reference to a baseline scenario for the Dutch economy. The baseline scenario is intentionally cautious, because it allows a 0.25 percentage point safety margin in the trend-based projection of annual economic growth. In line with the advice of the Social Economic Council (SER, 1998) and the Budget Study Group (Studiegroep Begrotingsruimte, 2001), this safety margin is smaller than the margins used in the cautious scenarios for the previous two government terms. Hence, there is a greater chance of setbacks than before, but it is still smaller than 50%.

The baseline scenario assumes no new policies. For government expenditures it follows the medium term projections of the Budget Memorandum 2002 (Tweede Kamer, 2001-2002). The important exceptions are those expenditure items that by nature, by law or by policy rule depend on specific macroeconomic variables: unemployment benefits, interest on government debt, and the level of government wages and social security benefits. For health care expenditure, the baseline scenario is derived from a forecast of supply and demand in the health care sector (CPB and SCP, 2001). Government receipts (mainly taxes and social security premiums) are estimated on the assumption of unchanged tax and premium rates.

Procedure

CPB assesses the economic effects of a policy programme only upon request of the party concerned. The official election programmes do not provide enough information for a proper analysis. For example, the official election programme may claim to spend more money on health care and education, but not specify the amounts of money involved, the time pattern or the allocation of funds towards *e.g.* an increase of the wage rates or a higher number of employees. Hence, CPB needs further explanation and details of the different policy ideas laid out in the programmes before it can start to make an assessment. Such information can only be provided by party representatives.

In 2001, eight parties asked for an assessment of the economic effects of their policy programmes for the 2002 general elections. With the elections scheduled for 15 May 2002, most political parties had drafts of their election programmes ready by October 2001.[1] On 1 November 2001, CPB published a new forecast for 2001-2002 and a week later it published the budgetary baseline for 2003-2006. The full baseline scenario was published by the end of November 2001.

Meanwhile, parties were asked to provide explanations and further details on the policy proposals in their election programmes. Just before the Christmas holidays, CPB provided each party with a first assessment of the budgetary effects. By mid-January, it also provided a first assessment of the macroeconomic effects and the income distribution. On the basis of these first assessments, parties had the opportunity to adjust the specifics of their policy proposals, so as to avoid undesired results or to improve on desired results. Based on revised specifications, CPB made a second assessment, and in early March 2002 it provided each party with a draft of the text about its programme for the final report. This included the text of an appendix specifying the policy proposals that were included in the analysis. Now parties could only correct apparent misunderstandings and give their reaction on the draft texts. CPB published the final report by the end of March 2002, seven weeks before the date of the elections.

Instruments

CPB's toolbox ranges from simple spreadsheets to fairly complex econometric models.[2] For budgetary accounting, a system of spreadsheets is used. But assessing the direct budgetary effect of a particular policy measure may require a thorough investigation of the subject matter at hand, as was the case for the various proposals to reduce the number of disability benefits. The workhorse for the macroeconomic analysis is the econometric model JADE of the Dutch economy.[3] Here again, a lot of work is spent on a correct translation of policy measures into model inputs. Indeed, to study the policy effects on labour supply, the MIMIC model is used (Graafland *et al.*, 2001), and its results are fed into the JADE analysis. The sectoral model Athena (Vromans, 1998) and a model of the energy market (Mannaerts *et al.*, 2002) are used to assess the impact of changes in the Regulatory Energy Tax. Sectoral results from the Athena model (Vromans, 1998) are also used as a check on the macroeconomic JADE results. Finally, a database of micro information on a large sample of households is used to assess the effects on purchasing power of different groups of households, thus providing information about the policy effects on the income distribution.

Misuse?

The operation of the models used by CPB is known, at least in broad outline, from previous CPB publications. It has been suggested in the media that the political parties make improper use of their knowledge of these models, by casting their programmes in such a way that they yield favourable model outcomes. Is this a valid point?

The answer to this question is twofold. In so far as the models offer a reasonable image of the actual relationships in the Dutch economy, such a use of model knowledge will lead to a more effective policy programme. There can be no suggestion of improper use here. Improper use would only occur if a party cleverly responded to a model's unrealistic characteristics. Such misuse must be prevented by a watchful CPB. Model outcomes should never be accepted unquestioningly, but always tested for realism. Thus the model users will expose any weaknesses in the model, which can then be corrected.

An example of potentially misleading results is provided by the standard purchasing power calculations for notional households. The most widely used analysis concentrates on purchasing power figures for standard households, the best known being that of the "standard employee" (*i.e.* earned income in the market sector just below the compulsory health insurance limit, non-working partner, two children, rented home, no special deductible items). There are no standard purchasing power figures in this publication, because they give an unbalanced view of the purchasing power effects flowing from the various election programmes. The implications for the income distribution are therefore illustrated in other ways.

Similarly, the standard indicator for business profitability is the complement of the labour income share. However, this indicator does not take into account possible changes in the corporate income tax. Because some party programmes contain a change in the corporate income tax rate, an adjusted indicator for profitability was used in CPB's list of target variables.

Dilemmas

The political parties and CPB face a number of dilemmas in the course of the exercise. They relate to the specification of the policy measures included in the analysis and to the presentation of the results and the public debate.

As mentioned above, CPB needs further explanation and details of the different policy ideas laid out in the election programmes before it can start to make an assessment. Such information is provided by party representatives and is published in an appendix to the final report. Whether the explanations and details given are actually in line with official party policy and remain consistent with the broader ideas of the programme, may sometimes be doubtful. However, CPB cannot and should not interfere with decision-making procedures of the different parties.

Part of the heavy workload of the entire exercise for CPB flows from the level of detail with which parties specify their policy measures in order to get an optimal result. CPB would rather focus on the main points, but who is to decide what the main points are? Similarly, a dilemma sometimes flows from the principle that policy measures can only be included if they fall under the power of national government. Measures which can only be taken in an international context, or which require policy changes by employers and trade unions or local authorities, are not taken into consideration. This principle reflects the fact the elections are for national parliament. Parties cannot get a better result because they intend to abolish national contributions to the European Union or because they expect the unions to settle for lower wage increases. But it is not always clear where to draw the line. In the 1998 programmes, several parties intended to reduce Dutch contributions to the EU. Within the rules of EU decision making, the national cabinet proved to have some power to block the level of contributions implied by the draft financial perspectives. And what to do with policy intentions to lower wage increases for government employees, or to reduce working hours in the government sector? Will the unions accept them, and if not, will the prospective government keep to its intentions when it faces strikes?

The final report intends to show how different parties propose to make different choices on the economic issues facing national policy making. This is underlined by the title of the report, "Charting choices". Everyone wants to take measures that cost nothing or have no down sides. But in practice everything has a price tag. As Milton Friedman titled a book famously, "There's no such thing as a free lunch" (Friedman, 1975). A party cannot raise public spending, cut taxes and reduce the public debt all at the same time. Another sphere where choices have to be made, is in the balance between additional economic growth and environmental objectives which cannot be expressed in money terms, such as the reduction of CO_2 emissions. A third example is the dilemma between income solidarity with benefit recipients and stimulation of participation in the labour market by reducing the replacement rate, that is, the ratio between the benefits for those out of work and the net pay of those in work.

Yet, a comparison of the numerical results on one or a few target variables tends to suggest that one or the other party has the better programme from an economic point of view. CPB has been looking for a graphical presentation that would offer a balanced view of the scores of the policy programmes in five or six relevant dimensions, one of them being a rest category which could be further explored for each party. An obvious choice is a cobweb diagram as used for instance by the European Commission to summarise multidimensional information[4], and by a Dutch consumer organisation in reporting product test results.[5] Unfortunately, for the present application we have not found an objective method to determine the measurement scales for the different axes.[6]

In spite of all the efforts of the CPB staff to write a balanced report and to provide a clear presentation, the results of the analysis may be misrepresented, accidentally or on purpose, in the public debate during the election campaigns. How should CPB react? We have chosen to refrain from public reactions at campaign time, unless we would signal a major misunderstanding.

4. WHY?

What are the merits of the exercise? What are the limitations? Why is this kind of analysis performed only in the Netherlands, and why by CPB?

Merits

As a result of the exercise, proposed policies are made specific and feasible, and the stated effects are made realistic. For participating parties it becomes very difficult if not impossible to make all kinds of promises that are unrealistic or not properly funded. In addition, the different policy programmes are made comparable. On previous occasions, the report has proved very helpful after the election for parties negotiating a coalition agreement, because it gives a ready comparison of similarities and differences in proposed economic policies.

The further elaboration and explanation which parties provide with their programmes creates greater clarity about the specific content of their policy proposals. Thus a party for instance cannot get away with vague indications about deep cuts with regard to disability benefits. The party will have to specify the kind of measures it wants to take, because it makes quite a difference whether it wants to change the benefit level, the eligibility criteria, or the premium differentiation. CPB also examines whether the various policy intentions are technically practicable and whether the resource allocations are realistic. The same measures have the same budgetary and economic effects, so that a party cannot arrive at more favourable results simply by being more optimistic about the effectiveness of the proposed policy.

The same baseline scenario as the starting point for the analysis applies to all parties. One party cannot boast better outcomes than another, simply by being more optimistic about economic developments under unchanged policies.

The uniform presentation of the policy proposals and their financial consequences make the parties' commitments in the financial and economic sphere mutually comparable. The use of clear demarcations of what is included in, say, "education", "safety" or "administration", reveals the differences and similarities between the parties in terms of the allocation of financial resources across the various policy areas.

In addition, CPB estimates the economic effects of the various policy packages. These projections sometimes induce parties to adjust their draft programmes. Juxtaposed, the estimated economic effects offer a picture of the choices that the parties are making with regard to the various social and economic issues. Where one party attaches great value to the level of benefits, another is willing to exchange these in part for higher GDP growth. Parties also strike different balances between, for instance, economic and environmental targets.

Limitations

The analysis also has some limitations. Not all policy intentions are easily translated into budgetary and economic effects, the figures suggest a precision that is not there, and election programmes deal with far more than just the economy.

As was mentioned above, for many policy proposals CPB considers the direct budgetary effects and the spending effects, but not what are known as the programme effects. Not enough is known about the economic effects of, for instance, more education, more public safety, or more infrastructure, leaving aside whether the proposed policies have been made sufficiently concrete. Incidentally, in many cases such programme effects will only become apparent after 2006.

The analysis is restricted to measures that can be taken within the next government's term of office and to their economic effects within that term. Especially when measures only have a gradual impact on the economy, the effects in the final year (2006) may still be relatively small. This has been accommodated to some extent by highlighting the effects on trend-based or potential growth as well as the effects on actual economic growth. The analysis is also limited to measures that the Dutch national government can take by itself. As said before, measures which can only be taken in an international context, or which require policy changes by employers and trade unions or local authorities, are not taken into consideration.

The quantitative analysis of the economic effects is surrounded by a number of uncertainties. The behavioural reactions of firms and households cannot be predicted accurately. However, the estimated effects of policy proposals are probably more reliable than the regular economic forecasts. The wide uncertainty margins surrounding the forecasts are to a large extent determined by uncertainties surrounding international developments. The policy effects are not, or only marginally dependent on international economic conditions. Even so, the results of the effect analysis should be treated as broad brush, and no great significance should be attached to small differences between parties. Meanwhile, I do not agree with those who claim that the differences in estimated economic effects between parties are (too) small. The difference in annual growth rate of potential GDP between VVD and GroenLinks is estimated at 0.7 percentage point, which is quite substantial: it amounts to 3% difference in the level of potential GDP after four years. Similarly, the difference in the equilibrium rate of unemployment between VVD and SP is 1% of the labour force, which can hardly be deemed small: it makes the difference between 310,000 or 400,000 unemployed.

The most important limitation of the CPB analysis is that the expected economic effects only touch on a few aspects of the wide-ranging political commitments contained in the election programmes. As mentioned, in a separate publication the RIVM deals with the expected effects of environmental policies. In addition, there are many other political objectives that are not taken into consideration in these analyses, like public safety or the social integration of immigrants.

Why in the Netherlands?

It is unique in the world that a single economic research institute performs a comparative economic analysis of the policy programmes of several political parties. Why would this occur in the Netherlands and not in other countries?

While I am probably not the best judge of this, let me offer two observations. First, Dutch political culture tends to go quite a long way in separating analytical questions from political preferences. There is a strong tradition of rationalism in politics.[7] Policy makers try to reach consensus on facts and use the best available knowledge to assess the effectiveness of different policy measures. Second, the multiparty system makes it more important to clarify the differences between the many parties and requires coalition building after the election. On both issues, the unbiased assessment of the economic effects of the different programmes is very helpful.

Why at CPB?

It is the task of CPB to make independent economic analyses and forecasts that are relevant for policy making. Hence, the requests from the parties to perform an economic analysis of their policy programmes call on CPB's core business. Also, in the Netherlands CPB is probably the only institute that is well-equipped to perform this type of analysis. It has a good knowledge of the government budget system, it maintains a number of econometric models of the Dutch economy and it has a long experience in analysing the economic effects of policy proposals.

Would it be a good idea to have other economic research institutes performing a similar analysis? This would certainly give more insight into the uncertainties that surround CPB's analysis. A second opinion is always helpful for a balanced assessment. But these advantages would come at high costs. One should consider not only the money costs of an additional exercise, but also the loss of clarity in communicating the results and the danger that parties would make selective use of the two (or more) analyses.

5. CONCLUSION

In my opinion, the balance of pros and cons indicates that the exercise is useful, because it helps to prevent false promises in election campaigns and provides relevant information on the political preferences of the different parties. At the same time, one should not exaggerate the value of the exercise and keep in mind the most important limitations: the fact that many policy targets are omitted and that the estimated economic effects carry substantial uncertainties.

NOTES

1 CPB published a preliminary budgetary baseline for 2003-2006 in June 2001, to provide some information to parties drafting the financial section of their programmes.
2 See also the contribution of Jacobs, Kuper and Sterken in this volume.
3 CPB (1997). More recent updates of the model will be documented shortly.
4 European Commission (2001), p. 77 *sqq*.
5 Consumentenbond, *Consumentengids* ("Consumer's Guide").
6 The 2002 report does contain cobweb diagrams for the qualitative analysis of the different proposals for reforming the health care system. Here, the measurement scales could be derived from the scores of the current system and the maximum possible scores on each dimension.
7 See CPB (1992), p. 95, and the references given there. See also the chapter by Den Butter in this volume.

REFERENCES

CPB (1986), *Macro-economische effecten van de verkiezingsprogramma's van PvdA, CDA en VVD* ("Macroeconomic Effects of the Election Programmes of PvdA, CDA and VVD"), Werkdocument/Working Paper 7, The Hague: CPB

CPB (1989), *Macro-economische effecten van de verkiezingsprogramma's 1990-1994 van CDA, PvdA, VVD en D66* ("Macroeconomic Effects of the Election Programmes 1990-1994 of CDA, PvdA, VVD and D66"), Werkdocument/Working Paper 32, The Hague: CPB

CPB (1992), *Nederland in Drievoud. Een scenariostudie van de Nederlandse economie 1990-2015.* ("The Netherlands in Triplicate. A Scenario Study of the Dutch Economy 1990-2015"), The Hague: Sdu Uitgeverij

CPB (1994), *Vijf verkiezingsprogramma's. Economische gevolgen van voorgenomen beleid* ("Five Election Programmes. Economic Effects of Proposed Policy"), The Hague: Sdu Uitgeverij

CPB (1997), *JADE, a Model for the Joint Analysis of Dynamics and Equilibrium,* CPB Working Paper 99, The Hague: CPB

CPB (1998), *Keuzes in kaart. Economische effecten van vijf verkiezingsprogramma's* ("Charting Choices. Economic Effects of Five Election Programmes"), The Hague: Sdu Uitgeverij

CPB (2002), *Keuzes in kaart 2003-2006. Economische effecten van acht verkiezingsprogramma's* ("Charting Choices 2003-2006. Economic Effects of Eight Election Programmes"), The Hague: CPB

CPB, RIVM, RPB, and SCP (2002), *Selectief investeren. ICES-maatregelen tegen het licht* ("Selective Investment. ICES Measures Held up to the Light"), The Hague: CPB

CPB and SCP (2001), *Een scenario voor de zorguitgaven 2003-2006* ("A Scenario for Health Care Expenditures 2003-2006"), CPB Document 7, The Hague: CPB

European Commission (2001), *European Competitiveness Report 2001*, Brussels: European Commission

Friedman, M. (1975), *There's no such Thing as a Free Lunch*, LaSalle Ill.: Open Court

Graafland, J.J., R.A. de Mooij, A.G.H. Nibbelink, and A. Nieuwenhuis (2001), *MIMICing Tax Policies and the Labour Market*, Amsterdam *et cetera*: North-Holland

Mannaerts, H.J.B.M., M.G. Lijesen, and M. Mulder (2002), *ELMAR: A Model of the European Electricity Market*, CPB Discussion Paper, forthcoming

SER (1998), *Advies Sociaal-economisch beleid 1998-2002* ("Advice Social Economic Policy 1998-2002"), Advice 98/08, The Hague: SER

Studiegroep Begrotingsruimte (2001), *Stabiel en duurzaam begroten* ("Stable and Durable Budgeting"), Report 11, The Hague: Ministerie van Financiën

Tweede Kamer (2001-2002), *Nota over de toestand van 's Rijks financiën. Miljoenennota 2002* ("Budget Memorandum 2002"), 28 000, nr. 1

Vromans, M. (1998), Athena. The Multi-Sector Model, *CPB Report*, 1998/3, 32-36

PART II

ECONOMIC METHODOLOGICAL ASPECTS

CHAPTER 4

FRANK A.G. DEN BUTTER

AN ECONOMIC PERSPECTIVE

1. INTRODUCTION

This chapter gives an economic perspective on the assessment of the election programmes by CPB Netherlands Bureau for Economic Policy Analysis (CPB). There are at least two ways for giving such economic perspective. The first way is to consider what body of economic knowledge is used in the assessment and to see whether the use of these economic methods is viable for the purpose of the exercise. In so far as this contribution takes this broad perspective, there is some overlap with the other chapters in this book. Another way is, however, to look at the assessment from a more narrow economic perspective, namely to consider the value of the exercise and to see whether its social benefits exceed the costs. In this chapter I will consider the CPB assessment mainly from the latter perspective, although I will not try to conduct a formal cost-benefit analysis. All-in-all it seems to me that this exercise adds enough value to the process of policy making as to be regarded as valuable. Yet it does not serve the most obvious purpose, namely that it helps the citizens of the Netherlands to decide about their votes.

The remainder of this chapter is organized as follows. The next section pictures the background of this unique exercise in the Netherlands and sketches the dilemma that conducting such an exercise poses to an independent government agency. Section 3 lists a number of reasons why such an exercise is valuable, both from the perspective of economic science and from the perspective of value added. Section 4 discusses some methodological problems of the assessment. Section 5 questions whether there should be a competition between various agencies and institutes in conducting this exercise. Finally, section 6 concludes.

Johan J. Graafland and Arie P. Ros (Eds.), Economic Assessment of Election Programmes: Does it Make Sense?, 33-44.

2. HISTORY AND BACKGROUND

The fact that it is the Netherlands where this unique assessment of election programmes is made, relates much to the institutional set-up of policy preparation in this country. In a way it can be seen as a modern spring-off of Tinbergen's theory of economic policy, where scientific insights on how instruments may affect policy goals are separated from political preferences on the trade-off between these goals. These ideas were, of course, very much inspired by the political and societal landscape in the Netherlands (see also Van Zanden, 2002, for a broad historic perspective). In the years just after World War II, when Tinbergen designed his theory of economic policy and was active in the institutional set-up of policy preparation in the Netherlands, the Dutch society was still very much pillarised. The four main pillars were the liberals, the Catholics, the Protestants and the socialists. Each of them were represented by one or more political parties with implicit preferences on policy goals in their own, so to say, social welfare function. As they all were minority parties, there has always been a need for the formation of a coalition government. The foremen of the political parties or pillars did realise that it was impossible to meet all of their own policy goals in such a coalition government. Although the pillarised society has changed very much since then and there has been a steady "depillarisation", still all parties are minority parties, even more so than before. Therefore the need for a compromise agreement for the coalition government has remained.

In the design of the policy preparation in the Netherlands, the analysis of CPB has always played a central role in these negotiations in what has become known as the Dutch polder model. As Tinbergen, who became CPB's first director in 1947, has built the first econometric policy model (Tinbergen, 1936), it is understandable that model based policy analysis has, from the origin, constituted an important part of the work of CPB. Its "model" early acquired a high status in academic circles and has come to be regarded in Dutch society as a more or less "objective" piece of economic science (Den Butter and Morgan, 1998). However, in the first few years of CPB there was a fierce internal discussion about the way the bureau should give shape to its advices.[1] On the one side was Van Cleeff, who had the view that CPB should follow a normative approach, while on the other side Tinbergen supported the idea of disentangling the positive and normative elements of the analyses. Crucial in this controversy was the question in which way economic policy advice would be the most successful in the pillarised economy. Van Cleeff tried to develop an all-embracing normative theory which would integrate the ideas of the different pillars. Tinbergen wanted to develop a method that would give the most objective description of reality. The differences between the pillars would then be minimised to their different normative proportions. In other words, he wanted to make a clear distinction between the workings of the economy (model) and the policy goals (welfare functions), and then "try to agree on the first and compromise on the second issue". Tinbergen won this battle. Since then, economic policy preparation in the Netherlands is organised in three autonomous parts: data, models and norms. The data and statistics are collected by the Central Bureau of Statistics (CBS), the workings of the economy are described by the models of CPB, and the balancing of different points of view is done by the government in dialogue with unions, employer organisations and other associations of organised interest. This method of splitting facts and politics has, up to now, always been a prominent feature in creating consensus in the Dutch society where all belong to a cultural minority or minority party.

The fact that the major political parties ask CPB to calculate the effects of their election programmes on economic growth, employment, income distribution and so on, seems almost a realisation of Tinbergen's dream to separate the knowledge on the working of the economy and the normative preferences on trade-offs between policy goals, which will differ for each political party (or pillar).

Given this historical background it is not remarkable that CPB conducts these assessments; it may be even more remarkable that it only started to do so in 1986. It should again be emphasised that CPB conducts the assessment at the *request* of the political parties and does not, apart from the timing of the exercise, take any initiative on its own. So it is the own will of the political parties whether they want their programme to be examined by CPB. In this way they aim to obtain the stamp of approval of CPB. Although there may be some herding involved in the decision of the political parties to participate (see the contribution of Van der Lecq in this volume) and although the smaller political parties complain that the exercise is relatively costly and time consuming for them, my impression is that the major political parties consider the assessment as useful, as it brings discipline and budgetary consistency when drafting the programme. In the larger political parties, with many hobby horses and shades of opinions between the active members, the assessment makes life easier for the person who has the responsibility for budgetary consistency of the program. So the financial spokesman of the Labour party (PvdA) discussed his input into the CPB assessment with two persons only, namely the political leader (Melkert) and the chairman of the party (Koole).[2]

Obviously, in a country where all economists have internalised Tinbergen's ideas of economic policy and Hennipman's thinking on welfare analysis, economic effects of the election programmes have been discussed by the profession long before CPB started with making the assessments. For instance, in 1972, the influential Dutch economic journal *Economisch Statistische Berichten* devoted a whole issue to the election programmes of the in those days seven largest political parties (ESB, 1972). It is interesting to see how the chief-editor of the journal, Hoffman (1972), anticipates on the need for the kind of assessment that CPB started fourteen years later. In his editorial, Hoffman states that economists can be helpful in their advice to politicians how they can best reach the policy goals. But then it is necessary that the political parties are clear about their policy goals (and about their trade-offs). According to Hoffman, in those days the political parties were not clear about these goals because in that case they had also to be clear about unpopular measures and about the price the public has to pay in order to reach these goals. Therefore Hoffman advocates an economic cost-benefit analysis in politics. In order to find out about policy goals and trade-offs, the contributions of the party experts in the special election edition of the journal in 1972 are centred around some specific questions in five policy fields. But the final assessment is still left to the readers of ESB.

Following this attempt of ESB to construct political welfare functions, and following the attempt by Van Eijk and Sandee (1959) of establishing a welfare function with the help of what that they call an imaginary interview with policy makers, Merkies (1973), in his inaugural lecture, tries to construct political welfare functions based on the answers of a questionnaire to the major political parties of those days. But his exercise is limited to the calculation of relative welfare gains for each party, given the actual values of the policy variables. So it can be seen which party has, according to its own welfare function, gained most welfare in the period under consideration. These exercises are still far away from the full assessment that CPB makes nowadays.

Yet, most of these predecessors are aware of the main dilemma that CPB faces in the assessment. On the one hand there is much value in obtaining quantitative information on effects of various policy proposals in the election programmes. However, a completely objective and politically unbiased judgement on these policy proposals can never be given. Although a good quantitative economist will conduct his analysis as objective as possible, a complete separation, as especially political scientists would emphasise, can never be made between analysis and normative preferences. It must be said that CPB has put much effort in the design of the assessment procedure to guarantee the unbiasedness of the outcomes, but the selection of the models and the input of much tacit human knowledge into the assessment (see Don's description of the procedure in this volume) will not completely prevent value judgement from creeping into the procedure. Therefore, apart from the value creating elements in the assessment, also some objections have been raised against this procedure.[3] The next two sections list both a number of the pros and cons of the assessment.

3. PROS

There are a number of reasons why the assessment exercise can be regarded as valuable. Some of these have already been alluded to in the previous sections. The first source of value of the exercise is that all policy proposals in the election programmes are calculated using the same model-based framework which is consistent with respect to national accounting at the macro level. It implies that the calculated effects on the policy goals are comparable for all political parties. In this way the assessment gives the impression of the implicit social welfare function of the various political parties. So the voters may decide which of the parties has a welfare function that concords most with their own preferences.

In fact the assessment procedure consists of three steps. The first step is that the political parties are confronted with the so-called baseline scenario, which assumes cyclical equilibrium at the end of the next period of government in 2006 (provided the government serves its full term).[4] The label "baseline" implies that trends in government expenditures in the main fields of policy concern (care, education, social security) have been extrapolated on the assumption of no additional policy efforts. So the policy proposals of the political parties are defined as changes with respect to trend growth implicit in this baseline scenario. It implies that, when the political parties propose a cut in spending in one policy field in order to be able to intensify expenditure in another policy field, it does not mean that there is an absolute decrease in spending in that first policy field, but only a relative decrease as compared to the baseline scenario. Of course this makes a careful wording of the assessment in the public debate necessary.

A second step in the assessment procedure is budgetary accounting. A definition equation describes in what way the political parties are planning to use the so-called "budgetary space" according to the baseline projection plus cuts in spending they propose. This use can be threefold, namely for additional spending, for reduction of the tax and premium burden, and for reduction of the government debt (where the norm is a one percent financial surplus in cyclical equilibrium in order to take the ageing of the population into account). Obviously this accounting rule is not based on model assumptions or on economic behaviour, and it contains no value judgement in that respect. It is noticeable that the rules and procedures for this budgetary accounting, including the norm for the budget surplus, are extensively discussed in policy advises of the Dutch Social Economic Council (SER) and in the so-called *Studiegroep Begrotingsruimte* ("Study Group Budgetary Space") which is a committee of high-ranked civil servants of ministries and of experts of the Central Bank on budgetary policy.

The working of the models and the assumptions on economic behaviour implicit in these models do play a major role in the third step of the assessment procedure. Here the effects of the policy proposals on the labour market, on product markets and on income distribution are calculated. There is, moreover, some feedback to the second step of the procedure as the model based exercise may yield negative or positive second-order effects on the government budget. However, in the most recent CPB assessment, the second-order effects are relatively small as compared to second-order effects found in previous assessment exercises (on which there has been much debate). It implies that in the exercise of this year the policy proposals of the political parties are, to a major extent, restricted by the static budget identity, given budgetary space in the baseline scenario.

Therefore, a second major advantage of the assessment procedure is that the political parties are forced to think about this budgetary consistency. It means that they have to be very strict on their proposals and cannot promise the moon at no costs. More in general, this discipline in making consistent policy plans can be regarded as a major value added in the use of models for economic policy analysis.[5] It does not only bring discipline in the policy plans, there is also ample interaction between the policy makers and the modelling experts on what kind of policy instruments are most effective in achieving the warranted policy goals. This interaction also occurs in the discussions of the CPB experts and designers of the election programmes of the political parties. Yet, the CPB's procedure is strict in the sense that the final outcome cannot be influenced by the political parties anymore. Moreover, during the procedure there is no information and discussion between the political parties about how they proceed in the assessment procedure and on the implementation of CPB of their policy proposals.

A third source of value of the assessment procedure is that the policy discussion takes place in line with CPB's belief on the working of the economy, which is based on sound and up to date economic theory, on empirical research and on a deep knowledge of economic institutions in the Netherlands. The policy analysis of CPB provides a kind of common language as framework for the policy discussions. This common language lowers the transaction costs in, *e.g.* the negotiations between the social partners. It is even remarkable how much, to give an example, the most recent advice of the Social Economic Council on medium term policy relies on studies conducted by CPB.[6] So the economic framework used in the assessment of the programmes of the political parties is familiar to all participants in the policy discussions in the Netherlands. They all speak, so to say, the language of CPB. Moreover, CPB has, in these circles, a high reputation for the quality of its analysis. It would take a long time for other institutes to build up a similar reputation. Because of the large investment costs in specific knowledge on this type of calculations, proliferation of such policy assessments of the election programmes would bring about huge costs, given the size of the Dutch economy. In this respect the Dutch situation cannot be compared with the German, which has six major institutes for economic policy analysis.

A final and most prominent source of value of the assessment is that the calculations contribute considerably to lowering the negotiation costs when after the elections a coalition government has to be formed. Due to the assessment, the negotiators in the formation process are aware of the effects which the proposals of the various election programmes have, according to the CPB calculations, on the policy goals. This has proven to be useful information in order to come to a compromise and reach a governmental agreement which consists of a combination of the most effective policy proposals from the programmes.[7] So, in an informal way, the assessment contributes to establish an overall social welfare function from the individual preferences of the political parties which constitute the government.

4. CONS

Most arguments in favour of the assessment of the programmes of the previous section also contain a seed from which doubt may grow on the value of the CPB exercise. It is already mentioned that it is impossible to calculate the effects of policy proposals in a completely objective way. There will always be normative aspects and some subjective interpretations in the implementation of the policy proposals in the modelling exercise. On previous occasions, as part of the learning process, there have been ample discussions between the makers of the programmes and the CPB staff on this implementation. In the recent exercise the room for these discussions has been restricted by keeping a tight time schedule. As yet, all three steps in the calculation procedure discussed in the previous section, contain elements of discretion. The basic scenario and the resulting calculation of the budgetary space is based on sound projections of structural growth, but, as a cautious trend projection underlies the scenario, the probability of a higher structural growth is larger than the probability of a lower one. It makes the basic scenario somewhat difficult to interpret. There is not much discretion in the second step, namely the budget constraint, where budgetary space plus cuts in spending should be equal to additional government expenditure plus tax reductions plus additional reduction of the government debt. However, the third step, where a mix of the CPB models is used for calculating the effects and propagation dynamics of the various policy proposals, is bound to many underlying assumptions. It may happen that the makers of the policy programmes disagree with the major mechanisms of the models used for the calculations. A first and not much complicated disagreement would be about calibrated or estimated values of the parameters of the models. The chapter by Graafland in this book shows that such differences in parameter values may already give rise to huge differences in the calculated effects of the policy proposals. A second and more fundamental disagreement would be about the dynamics of the model, namely the lag structure and the propagation speed of the policy proposals. This has been a cause of disagreement between the Christian Democratic CDA and CPB in the previous assessment of the election programmes in 1998.[8] The most serious objection of the designers of the policy programmes would be when they disagree with the working and specification of the model and its theoretical underpinning. In that case their request would be for the use of different model specifications.[9] All in all the political parties may ask for a sensitivity analysis with respect to this kind of specification changes. However, that would be very time consuming and would also involve the danger that the political parties go shopping for good results. Similarly I am afraid that the calculation of confidence intervals of the effects of the policy proposals by Monte Carlo simulations (as proposed by Graafland in this volume) would very much obscure the debate on the outcomes of the assessment.

Although ideally the assessment is to reveal the social welfare function of each political party, in reality the assessment exercise does not provide a clear-cut insight into the trade-offs between policy goals and into the preferences of the political parties. The outcomes are rather complicated in their mix of policy goals, input of various instruments and propagation dynamics. So some parties will have favourable effects on the short run, whereas their long-run economic performance is lower than that of other parties.[10] This rich diversity of outcomes makes it difficult to select the political party with preferences that come closest to one's own individual welfare function. That's why the assessment, apart from its technical character, is not very helpful to make laymen voters decide about their favourite party. CPB tries hard to present the outcomes in an opaque way, and all political parties will stress that their outcomes are the best, given their own criteria of judgements for the outcomes. On the other hand, the policy debate may be very selective with respect to the outcomes. It appears that the assessment of 2002 did not evoke such debate on specific outcomes, but on the occasion of previous assessment some major policy consequences, mainly with respect to the effects on employment, were very much blown up and put into the spotlight by the press and even by the leaders of the political parties. For instance in 1998, a leader of the (conservative) liberal VVD argued that the Christian Democrat CDA were not ready for government because their programme failed in enhancing employment. In the assessment of 2002 there were some misunderstandings in the press about the effect on purchasing power of lower and higher incomes, due to CPB's definition of lower and higher incomes where the class of higher incomes also comprised (lower) middle incomes.

Another problem with the assessment exercise, unavoidable though, is that the calculations of CPB are highly technical so that they are very difficult to judge for laymen and relative outsiders. It is really an insiders exercise, the scope of which can only be understood fully by experts. Moreover, it is questionably whether the results can be reproduced completely by outsiders.[11] In fact, the calculations are made by different models which generally do not yield the same impulse response effects. So a lot of not fully documented judgement is included in the exercise in combining the effects according to the various models.

A further source of distress on the exercise is that a number of aspects, which political parties (and the public!) may consider as important, cannot be taken into account in the calculations. These may be either positive effects, such as *e.g.* policy measures to enhance the quality of education, or to make the health system more efficient without additional expenditures, or negative effects of high transaction and transition costs that policy measures may bring about. In the latter case one can think of the costs of reliance on legal judgement with respect to proposals for immigration restrictions or for the reform of the disability act.[12] More in general, the assessment is confined to a quantification of the economic effects of the policy proposals. Although the assessment of 2002 has extended the analysis to a quality assessment with respect to the environment, the public health sector and disability, there is a danger that other important issues in the election campaign remain underexposed, such as values, norms and the preservation of social capital, safety and crime prevention, and government failure. The solution would be that the other planning bureaus would also make an assessment, albeit qualitatively, in their field of competence. As a matter of fact the RIVM, the Dutch National Institute of Public Health and the Environment, publishes its assessment in line with the CPB assessment.

A final and most interesting problem, or side effect of the assessment, is that the makers of the party programmes have become familiar with the properties of the models of CPB and will, in the policy proposals, see to it that they are effective in terms of the CPB models. In fact a bad performance in the CPB calculations, especially with respect to employment, has, on previous occasions, proved to lead to a loss of votes in the elections. The result is that this procedure generates those policy proposals of the political parties which are most beneficial according to the CPB models. So it has led to a remarkable convergence of policy plans, especially between the established parties, which would qualify for participation in the government. *E.g.*, in the assessment of 2002, the policy proposals of GroenLinks are so much in line with the proposals of the other parties that they were not excluded from taking part of the government by other parties on beforehand. This convergence may have contributed to the lack of interest of the Dutch population for general elections – apart from "depillarisation" which may be another cause. Moreover, there is a risk that the way the CPB models describe economic reality is not correct, so that all political parties are betting on the wrong horse in the design of their programmes. This would imply an extraordinary example of a political lock-in. It may even be a reason for the success of the political outsider Pim Fortuyn in 2002, who bluntly refused an assessment of the viability of his plans.

It is true that, as Don argues in his contribution to this book, it enhances welfare when the designers of the political programmes exploit the properties of the CPB models when these models give an adequate description of reality. However, the dominant role of the CPB models and their implicit conceptual framework with which all economists in the country have been educated, may have the danger of path dependency. Some kind of discourse coalition will emanate, which may exclude new and relevant conceptual ideas.[13] Yet it must be admitted that on one major occasion the change from Keynesian demand policy to neo-classical supply policy was initiated by CPB, and at first instance challenged by economists from academia.[14] On other occasions, the dominant framework of CPB policy analysis has indeed been challenged by outsiders.[15]

5. MONOPOLY VERSUS COMPETITION

As mentioned before, more competition in calculating the effects of the policy proposals in the election programmes is sometimes advocated as a way of overcoming the problem that the assessment is locked in too much in the modelling framework of CPB. More in general, CPB's reputation of independence has been challenged from time to time both in academia and by the press, especially with respect to its task of formal auditor for the government. Here the position of CPB is in fact that of a monopolist and it is true that CPB has a special position, as it has access to confidential information on government policy. This position is needed in order to be able to react promptly on questions by policy makers, which mainly regard technical and accounting aspects in policy discussions. Yet, in the institutional framework for policy making in the Netherlands, a number of checks and balances have been built in order to prevent CPB to misuse its monopoly position. Such misuse would also immediately destroy much of the reputation that the bureau has built up so carefully. Besides, as already mentioned, it is a question of efficiency to have, in a relatively small country as the Netherlands, only one institute which is responsible for this kind of macroeconomic forecasting and policy evaluations. This task requires a lot of specific investments and hence the institute has to be quite sizeable. It is typical for the institutional set-up of Dutch policy making that there are numerous formal and informal contacts between the CPB staff and the economists at ministries, researchers in academia and the staff of the social partners. On the one hand they provide relevant information to CPB, but, on the other hand, they will, if needed, be critical on CPB work. This argumentation also holds for the assessment of the election programmes.

CPB does not hold a monopoly position for its second task, namely that of institute of applied economic research. Here, it competes both with other Dutch institutes and with institutes abroad. Nowadays, CPB is asked more frequently than before to give a second opinion on research conduct by other institutes. In the same way, there is no objection that political parties ask second opinions on the effectiveness of parts of their programmes to other researchers, including research institutes at universities. Yet, a full economic assessment of the programmes in the way conducted by CPB, cannot be done by other institutes because of the costs involved in investments in specific knowledge and building up of reputation in the institutions of policy preparation in the Netherlands.

6. CONCLUSIONS

The assessment of the election programmes of political parties by CPB Netherlands Bureau for Economic Policy Analysis is unique in the world. Its background is the crucial role that the quantitative, model based economic analysis of CPB plays in the institutions of policy making in the Netherlands. The debate on economic policy proposals is organised in such a way that discussions on the working of the economy are, as much as possible, separated from the normative preferences with respect to policy goals. This way of organising the debate in, what is sometimes referred to as the "polder model", goes back to the ideas of Tinbergen on how to reach agreement between minority parties in a coalition government. The role of CPB is to provide a scientifically sound and well-respected analysis of actual economic developments and of best guesses of the effects of policy measures. CPB has made so much specific investments in this type of policy analysis, and has built up such good reputation of being independent, that the assessment of the election programmes proves valuable in the policy debate. The assessment generates value, not only for the political parties, who are forced to be consistent and explicit in their policy proposals, but also for the country as a whole. The latter is true, not so much because the assessment may articulate the preferences of the voters, but mainly because it proved very helpful in drafting the agreements of the coalition governments.

Of course, the assessment procedure also has its drawbacks. In reality, an "objective" computation of impulse response effects of the various policy measures proposed by the political parties is impossible. There is always some discretion in the interpretation and implementation of the policy proposals by the CPB staff. The models which are used in the exercise, although well-documented and eclectic in their theoretical background, contain many assumptions on the working of the economy which may be challenged by the experts of the parties. Moreover, the assessment uses different models where the outcomes do not fully accord, so that there is also some discretion in bringing the outcomes in line with each other. Another objection raised to the exercise is that political parties learn to exploit the mechanisms built into the models, and that policy measures which fall outside the scope of CPB's modelling exercise and do not obtain CPB's "stamp of approval", will not be taken seriously in the policy making process (Review Committee CPB, 1997).

This possible lock-in into the dominant economic discourse coalition can be avoided when a more broad and qualitative analysis is made of those policy proposals in the election programmes which cannot be implemented in the modelling exercise, and which have no major budgetary consequences. One can think of judgement by independent experts with various disciplinary backgrounds, but also of an assessment by the other "planning agencies", such as Social and Cultural Planning Bureau, and the newly-found Spatial Planning Bureau.

More in particular, with respect to the discretion in the assumptions and implementation in the modelling exercise, a supervisory committee of independent technical experts could be helpful in steering the discussions between the CPB staff and the makers of the election programmes. This committee could write a report of its own with annotations and critical remarks on the assumptions made in the assessment exercise. Moreover, CPB could report on a sensitivity analysis with respect to some of the crucial assumptions of the calculations, and of the way policy proposals are implemented in the models. Yet such publication of a range of outcomes for the policy goals would further obscure the public debate on the proposals. It also comprises the danger that the political parties will go shopping for assumptions (and modelling structure) that is most favourable to their proposals.

Finally, it would be useful to conduct a post mortem analysis of the previous assessment of the election programmes. Of course, such post mortem cannot establish the quality of the assessment, but it may be interesting to confront the plans of the political parties in the previous elections with the actual outcomes after the period of government. How much of the plans have been realised, what effects can be attributed to the policy measures which were actually taken, and how much of economic developments can just be ascribed to external factors? Such a post mortem could put in perspective the relative importance of policy proposals in election programmes, and hence the weight that should be attached to the assessment of these proposals.

NOTES

1 See Van den Bogaard, 1998.
2 See De Kam (2002), and the chapter by Van Liedekerke in this volume.
3 See *e.g.* Review Committee CPB (1997).
4 In 2002, this condition was violated within six months.
5 See *e.g.* Den Butter and Morgan (2000).
6 See SER (2002).
7 See Compaijen and Den Butter (1996), for a comparison of programmes and the governmental agreement of 1994.
8 See Verbon (1998), and Don (1998).
9 See the survey by Jacobs *et al.* in this book on various types of models used for policy analysis.
10 See also the discussion in this book by Jacobs *et al.* on the dynamic budget constraint.
11 See also the chapter by Graafland in this volume.
12 See Hazeu and Den Butter (2002), and the chapter by Bomhoff and Van der Geest in this volume.
13 See Van den Bogaardt (2002).
14 See Den Hartog and Tjan (1974, 1976), Driehuis and Van der Zwan (1978), and Den Butter (1991).
15 See *e.g.* Van Bergeijk and Van Sinderen (2000).

REFERENCES

Bergeijk, P.A.G. van, and J. van Sinderen (2000), Models and Macroeconomic Policy in the Netherlands, in F.A.G. den Butter and M.S. Morgan (Eds.), *Empirical Models and Policy Making: Interactions and Institutions*, London: Routledge, 26-38

Bogaard, A.A. van den (1998), *Configuring the Economy. The Emergence of a Modelling Practice in the Netherlands, 1920-1955*, Amsterdam: Thela Thesis

Bogaard, A.A. van den (2002), *De verwevenheid tussen toekomstverkenning en beleid; het ontstaan van vertoogcoalities ("The Interwovenness of Exploration of the Future and Policy; The Rise of Discourse Coalitions")*, Working Document W127, Scientific Council for Government Policy (WRR), The Hague: WRR

Butter, F.A.G. den (1991), Macroeconomic Modelling and the Policy of Restraint in the Netherlands, *Economic Modelling*, 8(1), 16-33

Butter, F.A.G. den, and M.S. Morgan (1998), What Makes the Models-Policy Interaction Successful?, *Economic Modelling*, 15(3), 443-475

Butter, F.A.G. den, and M.S. Morgan (Eds.) (2000), *Empirical Models and Policy Making: Interactions and Institutions*, London: Routledge

Compaijen, B., and F.A.G. den Butter (1996), *De Nederlandse Economie 2: Algemeen- en financieel-economische beleidsanalyse* ("The Dutch Economy 2: General- and Financial Economic Policy Analysis"), Groningen: Wolters-Noordhoff

Don, F.J.H. (1996), De positie van het Centraal Planbureau ("The Position of the Central Planning Bureau"), *Economisch Statistische Berichten*, 81(4048), 208-212

Don, F.J.H. (1998), Verbons verwijten aan CPB onterecht ("Verbon's Reproach at CPB Unjust"), *Christen Democratische Verkenningen*, nr. 9/10, 406-410

Driehuis, W., and A. van der Zwan (Eds.) (1978), *De voorbereiding van het economisch beleid kritisch bezien* ("The Preparation of Economic Policy Critically Considered"), Leiden: Stenfert Kroese

Eijk, C.J. van, and J. Sandee (1959), Quantitative Determination of an Optimum Economic Policy, *Econometrica*, 27(1), 1-13

ESB (1972), Economische visies van politieke partijen ("Economic Views of Political Parties"), *Economisch Statistische Berichten,* 57(2874), 1060-1079 (with contributions by J.M. den Uyl – PvdA, M.J.W.M. Peijnenburg – KVP, G.M.V. van de Aardenne – VVD, A. Schouten and A.J. Vermaat – ARP, H.A.F.M.O van Mierlo – D'66, D.F. van der Mei and N.C. de Ruiter – CHU, and W. Drees jr.- DS'70)

Hartog, H. den, and H.S. Tjan (1974), *Investeringen, lonen, prijzen en arbeidsplaatsen* ("Investment, Wages, Prices and Jobs") CPB Occasional Paper No. 2, The Hague: CPB

Hartog, H. den, and H.S. Tjan (1976), Investment, Wages, Prices and Demand for Labour (a Clay-Clay Vintage Model for the Netherlands), *De Economist*, 124(1/2), 32-55

Hazeu, C.A., and F.A.G. den Butter (2002), Een WAO die werkt: prikkels in plaats van arbitrage ("A Working Disability Act: Incentives Instead of Arbitration"), *Economisch Statistische Berichten*, 87(4349), 164-167

Hoffman, L. (1972), Politiek in ESB ("Politics in ESB"), *Economisch Statistische Berichten*, 57(2874), 1057

Kam, C.A. de (2002), Verslingerd aan het Planbureau ("Mad About CPB"), *NRC-Handelsblad*, 23 April, 16

Merkies, A.H.Q.M. (1973), *Van prognoses naar programma's* ("From Prognoses to Programmes"), Inaugural lecture, Amsterdam: Vrije Universiteit

Review Committee CPB (1997), *Scanning CPB: A View From the Outside*, The Hague: CPB

SER (2002), *Advies Sociaal-economisch beleid 2002-2006* ("Advice Social-Economic Policy 2002-2006"), No. 2002/08, The Hague: SER

Tinbergen, J. (1936), Kan hier te lande, al dan niet na Overheidsingrijpen, een verbetering van de binnenlandse conjunctuur intreden, ook zonder verbetering van onze exportpositie? Welke lering kan ten aanzien van dit vraagstuk worden getrokken uit de ervaringen van andere landen? ("Is a Recovery in the Domestic Economic Situation of this Country Possible, with or without Action on the Part of the Government, even without an Improvement in our Export Position? What Can be Learnt about this Problem from the Experience of Other Countries?"), in: *Praeadviezen voor de Vereeniging voor de Staathuishoudkunde en de Statistiek*, The Hague: Nijhoff, 62-108

Verbon, H.A.A. (1998), Vernieuwing van de partij – CPB modellen verwijtbaar ondeugdelijk ("Renewal of the Party – CPB Models Reproachable Unsound"), *Christen Democratische Verkenningen*, nr. 7-8, 345-349

Zanden, J.L. van (2002), Driewerf hoera voor het poldermodel ("Three Cheers for the Polder Model"), *Economisch Statistische Berichten*, 87(4358), 344-347

CHAPTER 5

J.P.A.M. (JAN) JACOBS, GERARD H. KUPER AND ELMER STERKEN*

MACRO MODELS AS WORKHORSES

1. INTRODUCTION

Macroeconomists are aware of the fact that a single model cannot fulfil all "goals" of macro modelling: (1) describe the (recent) past, (2) forecast future developments, and (3) carry out policy analysis. The work by Lucas (1976) typically initiated a departure from the notion that one full-fledged model could be used to reach these multiple goals. Apart from the new-classical critique, some economic schools advocated that models could not be used at all to analyse macroeconomic phenomena and/or decision-making. Some economists did so before Lucas presented his critique, but were only acknowledged thereafter. The (neo-) Austrian school for example had no confidence at all in modelling macroeconomic events or policy decision-making.[1] The argument is simple. In a macroeconomic system, billions of economic agents interact. Modelling these decisions is impossible, certainly if one believes that agent A's decisions depend on agent B's plans. Post-Keynesians, a radical Keynesian school, gave a similar argument – but from a very different perspective. Both lines of thought are/were however not supported at a large scale, contrary to the third one, the new-classical critique, which is certainly adopted in mainstream economics.

How did macro modellers respond to the fierce new-classical critique? Two main reactions can be observed. On the one hand, academic macroeconomists tried to meet the Lucas critique by including forward-looking behaviour in their models. They also (partially) abandoned the so-called Cowles Commission approach by avoiding imposing economic structure on macro-econometric systems. In the Cowles tradition, economic theory is used to impose *a priori* restrictions on the endogeneity of the key variables in macro systems. Next, macroeconomists partly

Johan J. Graafland and Arie P. Ros (Eds.), Economic Assessment of Election Programmes: Does it Make Sense?, 45-59.

switched from statistical to more theoretical general equilibrium models. In addition, microeconomic foundations of macro models became very popular. Ultimately, these developments led to an almost standstill in the traditional academic business of macro-econometric policy analysis, the exception perhaps being the work of the ESRC Macroeconomic Modelling Bureau at the University of Warwick.[2] On the other hand, macroeconomists in government agencies gradually switched from a single large-scale macro-econometric system to "suites" of models, families of single-purpose models ("workhorses") not necessarily linked to each other. Holding a portfolio of models (a "stable") makes one less vulnerable for critique, but creates consistency problems in-house, since all the horses need to be trained for different courses.

Which route has our profession taken from here? In this chapter, we address this question. Implicitly we will argue that it is the task of macroeconomists to advise the public on future developments and (policy) alternatives. The problem is how to organise and monitor this activity. There is public demand for forecasts and policy advice that the market cannot offer at high quality. The government is responsible for offering this public good, but a serious co-ordination problem exists here. In the Netherlands, the main solution to this co-ordination problem was the establishment of CPB Netherlands Bureau for Policy Analysis (CPB), previously the Central Planning Bureau, just after World War II. CPB plays a key role in producing macro-economic forecasts and in analysing policy alternatives. The latter task is the main subject of this chapter. We discuss various methods to analyse election programmes of political parties. CPB analyses these election programmes about six months prior to each Dutch election, its latest publication being *Keuzes in Kaart 2003-2006* (CPB, 2002).

Section 2 reviews the type of models one can use to describe macroeconomic systems, to forecast future developments, and to provide policy advice. Section 3 compares the current CPB models with our classification and assesses CPB's latest policy analysis exercise *Keuzes in Kaart 2003-2006*. Section 4 illustrates two of our main points of critique: (i) forward-looking behaviour and the intertemporal government budget constraint and (ii) the use of density forecasts to express forecast uncertainty. Section 5 concludes.

2. MODERN MACRO WORKHORSES

In the old days, the macroeconomist placed his bet on one horse. This horse, a standard Keynesian IS-LM-AS type model, was bred in the Cowles Commission tradition. Nowadays he/she owns a stable with different horses to satisfy macro-modelling demands. We will review modern macro instruments focusing on the three traditional goals of modelling: describing the past, forecasting the future and analysing policy scenarios.

Descriptive models

We select some of the models from the recent macroeconomic textbook of Heijdra and Van der Ploeg (2002):

- Short-run fluctuations are modelled with New-classical Real Business Cycle models or New-Keynesian updates of the (open economy) IS-LM-AS model. These updates use ingenious tricks to include imperfections, like nominal price rigidities, restrictions to trade (*e.g.* OverLapping Generation (OLG) Models) or other forms of rigidities (prices, wages and/or expectations).
- Modelling long-term economic growth usually starts from the Ramsey model (or a similar general equilibrium model). Alternatively, the OLG-class of models is employed. In all cases, an explicit treatment of consumer and producer behaviour is essential.

Forecasting models

Pagan and Robertson (2000) review the state of the art in macroeconomic forecasting models and distinguish six types of models:

- *"Core" Macroeconomic Models.* These systems of about 30 key variables and around 100-150 identities generally start from "sensible" long-run relations with some equilibrium correcting mechanism. Some of the models are econometric (the Norwegian model RIMINI), others are more based on theory (the calibrated Canadian QPM). This class of models shows the remainders of the old Tinbergen-Klein or Cowles Commission models.
- *Vector Auto Regressions (VAR).* Unlike the models in the previous class, these models do not make *a priori* distinctions between endogenous and exogenous variables. A limited number of variables are explained by their own past. These systems are primarily used in forecasting, but have turned to policy analysis instruments in recent days (Jacobs and Wallis, 2002). In order to be suited for policy analysis, VAR models require structure in the form of identifying assumptions (Cooley and Leroy, 1985), hence the label Structural VAR (SVAR) models for the second generation of VAR models.
- *Small Forward-Looking Models.* These models coincide with the theoretical short-run IS-LM-AS models mentioned earlier.[3] Their focus is on the forward-looking IS-curve and the wage-price model. Given their theoretical nature these models are not suited for short-run forecasting.
- *Single Equation Regression Models.* These reduced-form econometric models are used for the analysis of the Phillips-curve or the exchange rate in economies under floating regimes.
- *Dynamic Equilibrium Models.* This class finds its foundation in equilibrium business cycle models (or growth models). Econometric models always suffer from the fact that coefficients are functions of underlying preferences and technology, and more importantly, government policy. Changes in policies should therefore lead to changes in coefficients, which is typically not accounted for in reduced-form econometric models. Dynamic (Stochastic General) Equilibrium models are able to analyse policy changes or changes in tastes and technology. An example is the G-cubed model of McKibbin and Wilcoxen (1999).
- *Business Cycle Indicator Models.* In fact, these models are single-equation (or a limited number of equations) econometric time-series models. Economic theory

is not prominent, but the matching of moments of time series is. For an example, see Jacobs (1998).

Policy analysis models

Most of the above types of models can also be used for policy analysis, but some are better equipped. Policy analysis is an art, rather than a mechanical exercise. In most cases, one requires that a model is able to produce sensible forecasts prior to the use of scenario analysis. Moreover, even more than in the other modelling activities the craftsmanship of the modeller is crucial. How is the policy experiment set up? Which model variables are perturbed? Is the alternative policy consistent with other assumptions?

The most prominent classes of models that are used in policy analysis are (note the similarity with the forecasting classes):

- *"Core" Macroeconomic Models.* A nice example is COMPACT (Wren-Lewis *et al.*, 1996 and Darby *et al.*, 1999). This New-Keynesian model has classical long-run properties (money being neutral), medium-term (vintage-type) frictions and short-run nominal rigidities (with forward-looking wage-price setting). The model contains about 20 estimated equations.
- *Structural Vector Auto Regressions.* The SVAR models in this class are basically identical to the SVAR models we discussed in the forecasting classification. A prominent recent example is the Cambridge long-run structural co-integrating VAR model of the U.K. (Garratt *et al.*, 2002). This model is a Vector Error Correction Model (VECM) that includes long-run structural relationships derived from economic theory as long-run or co-integrating relations.
- *Small Forward-Looking Models.* An example is the Batini and Haldane (1999) model, as operated by the Bank of England (1999). This model is used to check the results of policy simulation experiments obtained by the econometric models of the Bank of England. Hargreaves's (1999) model of New Zealand is another example.
- *Dynamic Equilibrium Models.* This wide class of models includes highly theoretical Dynamic Stochastic General Equilibrium models, Deterministic Equilibrium Models, and Applied General Equilibrium Models. These subclasses vary in their purposes. Applied General Equilibrium Models concentrate on heterogeneity of agents, while Stochastic models focus on *e.g.* asset prices and interest rate shocks.
- *Scenario Models.* These models are sketchier and certainly not founded in serious econometrics. They are generally used to analyse institutional change. What are *e.g.* the consequences of downgrading of tastes? What is the impact of *e.g.* the New Economy on production structures? RIVM (2002), the accompanying study to *Keuzes in Kaart 2003-2006*, fits into this class.

The model classes presented above vary from theoretical frameworks to high-tech econometric systems. All have advantages and flaws. What are the pros and cons of these various classes? This is no easy question to answer. Table 1 summarises the relative strengths by stating in which cases the models can be applied.

Table 1 Which models have to be used in policy analysis?

Type of analysis	*Type of model*
Short-run multipliers	Core Macroeconomic Models Small Forward-Looking Models SVAR Models
Fiscal reform	(Applied) Dynamic Equilibrium Models
Monetary policy	Small Forward-Looking Models
Demographic analysis	Dynamic Equilibrium Models (OLG Models)
Environmental policy	(Applied) Dynamic Equilibrium Models Scenario Models
Institutional reform	(Applied) Dynamic Equilibrium Models Scenario Models

- *Short-run multipliers*: what are the consequences of next year's increase in the growth rate of world trade or similar (macroeconomic) shocks? Analysing short-run multipliers requires having to cope with the following macroeconomic themes: (i) short-run nominal rigidities, (ii) forward-looking – but not necessarily rational – behaviour of agents, (iii) fiscal and monetary closure rules (how will monetary and fiscal authorities respond to the shock?), and (iv) dynamics or econometric estimates of lag structures. The Core Models are appropriate for this exercise, as well as the class of Small Forward-Looking Models. The former category probably contains more likely candidate variables to "play around" with. SVAR Models also meet the requirements and are to be preferred to the Core Models. Econometric models have an additional advantage: they can be used to produce outcomes with confidence intervals or density forecasts of most likely outcomes. Dynamic Equilibrium Models are less suited for this type of policy analysis.
- *Fiscal reform*: what is the impact of a tax increase or a change in the tax mix (*e.g.* from direct to indirect taxes)? Core Models cannot be employed for this type of experiment, although they are probably needed to produce input for a more detailed equilibrium analysis (by "guesstimating" the macro impact of tax changes). Because Core Models typically do not distinguish heterogeneous agents, income distribution effects of fiscal reforms cannot be assessed. SVAR Models typically have a limited number of model variables, which disqualifies them for a detailed fiscal analysis. The best candidates for fiscal policy analysis are (Applied) Dynamic Equilibrium Models.
- *Monetary policy*: how is an interest rate change transmitted? This type of question is best analysed by the class of the Small Forward-Looking Models, since they often include monetary reaction functions. Most Core Models and SVAR Systems do not contain interest rate feedback rules, which are needed for this type of analysis.

- *Demographic analysis*: what is the impact of ageing? Here we can only use Dynamic Equilibrium (Optimising) Models, with the requirement of explicit recognition of heterogeneity in population age (OLG models). The other models are not decently equipped for this task
- *Environmental policy*: what is the impact of reducing the use of private transportation? None of the econometric models seems to be capable of analysing the consequences of environmental policy reform, although Dynamic Equilibrium Models could be employed to adjust utility and technology functions (and optimise them under new binding constraints). Scenario Models can be used, but have the well-known problems with respect to inference.
- *Institutional reform:* what are the consequences of moving from a pay-as-you-go social security system to a fully funded system? Dynamic Equilibrium Models and Scenario Models are the proper instruments to address this topic too. Various problems hamper the translation of these kinds of fundamental policy changes into macro model assumptions. First, how do these changes affect tastes and technologies? Second, how do forward-looking agents respond? Since many of these policies focus on the long run, it is hard to give a time-consistent response trajectory of the implied changes.

So, there does not exist an overall dominant class of models. This is the main motivation to maintain a "stable" or portfolio of various types of models to meet various goals.

3. THE CPB MODELS

The previous section reviewed the macroeconomic horse stable. It is an impressive stable, and if one wants to breed and look after all "horses" it can become quite expensive. This section discusses the CPB models and the apparent choices CPB made to keep the stable manageable. After that, we investigate the CPB models in more detail, focusing on policy analysis. We do not dive into the rich history of the macro-econometric model building tradition at CPB. Interested readers are referred to *e.g.* Broer *et al.* (1998) for a brief overview.

CPB operates the following models:

- The Core Macroeconomic Model *JADE*: Joint Analysis of Dynamics and Equilibrium.[4] This working horse is an annual econometric model that combines a consistent long-run model (found using co-integration techniques) with short-run fluctuations (in an error-correction framework). The model contains more variables than usual in Core Models (over 2,000) and can generate projections over 15 years. It has some nice theoretical features, like monopolistic goods markets, wage bargaining, and labour matching. The model operators are able to combine (outcomes of) this model with the two other models (the firm-sector model *ATHENA* and the Applied General Equilibrium Model *MIMIC*, see hereafter) in policy simulations.
- The multi-sectoral model *ATHENA* (Vromans, 1998). This model distinguishes fifteen branches of industry and is used in short- en medium-term analyses. Policy experiments, like different taxes or new infrastructure projects, can be

analysed. It is a Core Model with more sectoral detail (and therefore operated in combination with *JADE*). At present, *ATHENA* is under construction to enable long-term projections.

- The short-run *SAFE* model: Short-term Analyses and Forecasts for the Dutch Economy (Donders and Lunsing, 1999). This quarterly econometric model is used for one to three-year forecasts on a quarterly frequency. Although not as elaborated (*e.g.* no distinction between sheltered and exposed sectors and no modelling of supply), it resembles *JADE*. The wage equation is similar to the *JADE* wage equation. *SAFE* is mainly used to generate short-run forecasts for CPB's biannual projections.
- A model of the energy market, *ELMAR* (Mannaerts *et al.*, 2002). This model is used to assess the impact of changes in the Regulatory Energy Tax in combination with the sectoral model *ATHENA*.
- The Applied General Equilibrium model *MIMIC*: the Micro Macro model to analyse the Institutional Context.[5] This static model is the main response of CPB to the Lucas critique. The model derives supply and demand equations from optimising individual agents. It contains fifteen thousand variables, and distinguishes 6 production sectors and 40 types of households. This makes the model suited to analyse welfare effects and all kinds of fiscal and income policies. *MIMIC* is operated in combination with *JADE*.
- The CPB *Business Cycle Indicator* (Kranendonk and Jansen, 1997). This is basically a statistical model that denotes the current state of the economy and predicts short-run fluctuations.
- *WORLDSCAN* (CPB, 1999). This model, an Applied General Equilibrium Model that focuses on growth and trade, is used to analyse global policy changes at the world level. This type of analysis is essential to arrive at consistent projections for the Dutch economy.

How does the CPB stable compare to international standards? Table 2 compares the CPB models to the classification scheme of the previous section.

The first observation from Table 2 is that CPB typically neglects smaller-scale systems. We will argue below that this is a serious omission, although the choice can be justified by the specific role of CPB in economic policy advising in the Netherlands. CPB is obliged to present detailed policy analyses like the evaluation of election programmes, for which simple small-scale models are useless. On the other hand, small-scale systems might be used to explain difficult theoretical notions to a non-professional audience. What are the key mechanisms that determine economic development in the Netherlands? Therefore, either a SVAR System or a Small Forward-Looking Model would be helpful and valuable, especially in eliciting big macro differences between various policy alternatives.

Table 2 The CPB models

Descriptive	*Forecasting*	*Policy analysis*	*CPB models*
IS-LM-AS models			-
	Core Macroeconomic Models	Core Macroeconomic Models	JADE SAFE ATHENA ELMAR
	(Structural) Vector Auto Regressions	(Structural) Vector Auto Regressions	-
	Small Forward-Looking Models	Small Forward-Looking Models	-
	Single Equation Regression Models		-
	General Equilibrium Models	General Equilibrium Models	MIMIC
	Business Cycle Indicator		CPB Indicator
		Scenario Models	WORLDSCAN

Secondly, the CPB Core Models have relatively strong econometric foundations. Compared with foreign modelling experience there is a relative preference for the econometric approach. In *JADE* econometric results determine the long run, while the idea that economic theory dominates the precise formulation of long-run relations is more standard. This is certainly no disqualification; the CPB model builders surely know how to calibrate their models in order to get sensible outcomes.

Thirdly, the CPB Core Models ignore forward-looking behaviour.[6] In general, there seems to be a disinterest in asset markets and asset pricing, including monetary relations. The Netherlands being a small open economy, a Dutch model building institution cannot be blamed too much. However, ignoring forward-looking behaviour may blur the analysis of economic policy measures that have an alleged impact on financial markets.

Fourthly, the main fiscal policy variables are exogenous, so fiscal closure is not guaranteed. This can be – and probably is – done by hand, but ignoring forward-looking behaviour and the dynamic government budget constraint can lead to projections that are hard to interpret. This point is illustrated in Section 4 below.

Finally, the CPB does not present uncertainty measures. Model outcomes, especially forecasts, are subject to uncertainty.[7] Public discussion often focuses on point forecasts. Although some institutions like CPB report outcomes of "high" and "low" scenarios, for the model user it is valuable to know the probabilities of these outcomes. An econometric analysis allows combining the effects of future random shocks, coefficient estimation error and uncertainty in exogenous variable projections into an estimate of the uncertainty that surrounds a point forecast. A complete density forecast can be provided if one adds distributional assumptions (Wallis, 2000). The main reason for neglecting uncertainty is probably the scale of the models. As mentioned earlier, a smaller model allows precise density forecasts of the key variables (GDP growth, inflation and unemployment). "High" and "low" scenarios can also be expressed in terms of density intervals. For politicians this would not be of much help, but for the model users and analysts it would imply a big improvement. Section 4 gives an illustration.

All these issues affect the discussion of the evaluation of election programmes, like in *Keuzes in Kaart 2003-2006* (CPB, 2002). Small-scale systems could stimulate the thinking of the general audience, especially in an election campaign. The lack of a theoretical long-run equilibrium devaluates the usefulness of the Core Models for longer-horizon analyses. The main simulations that underpin the analysis of election programmes are carried out using *JADE* as the prominent working horse. This econometric model ignores the impact of policy measures on deep structural parameters (such as the parameters in the utility functions or technology functions). The model parameters need not be invariant to these policy shocks. Since forward-looking decisions in the government sector are also absent, the intertemporal government budget constraint is not modelled explicitly, which might lead to dynamic inconsistencies. Here one could object that the model forecasts only run until 2006. But even in a period of four years dynamic inconsistencies can lead to serious problems. The CPB discusses the uncertainty of the most likely scenario, but avoids a discussion on the uncertainty of the analysis of the policy proposals. The models used could be too large to calculate confidence intervals or it might be impossible to come up with probability functions. The alternative of using smaller models is not feasible, since these models are typically not suited for policy analyses. However, there is an alternative: stochastic simulation (Fair, 1994). It is intellectually challenging – and revealing to the general public – to judge whether the real wage increase of single-income households according to political party A would still be higher than the one initiated by party B at for instance the 90-percent confidence level.

4. ILLUSTRATIONS

In this section we present two illustrations of our main points of criticism on the ability of the CPB models to give an appropriate evaluation of policy proposals in election programmes: (i) the dynamic budget constraint, and (ii) the use of fan charts in representing uncertainty.

The dynamic budget constraint

Suppose we have a government sector that decides in period t on expenditure G_t, taxes T_t and the issuing of government debt B_t (all variables in nominal terms). The government budget identity then reads in nominal terms:

$$G_t + i_{t-1}B_{t-1} = T_t + (B_t - B_{t-1}) \tag{1}$$

where i_t is the nominal interest rate. In terms of fractions of nominal GDP (P_ty_t, where P_t is the general price level and y_t is real GDP), this equation reads:

$$\frac{G_t}{P_t y_t} + i_{t-1}\frac{B_{t-1}}{P_t y_t} = \frac{T_t}{P_t y_t} + \frac{B_t}{P_t y_t} - \frac{B_{t-1}}{P_t y_t} \tag{2}$$

Suppose π is the rate of inflation and λ is the growth rate of real GDP. Defining $b_t=B_t / P_ty_t$, $g_t=G_t / P_ty_t$ and $t_t=T_t / P_ty_t$ it can easily be seen that (2) equals:

$$g_t + \left[\frac{(1+i_{t-1})}{(1+\pi)(1+\lambda)} - 1\right]b_{t-1} = t_t + b_t - b_{t-1} \tag{3}$$

We define the real interest rate by: $r=i-\pi$, and assume the interest rate to be constant, so the term between square brackets is by approximation equal to $r-\lambda=h$, so we get:

$$g_t + hb_{t-1} = t_t + b_t - b_{t-1} \tag{4}$$

We solve equation (4) forward in time:

$$(1+h)b_{t-1} + \sum_{k=0}^{\infty}\frac{g_{t+k}}{(1+h)^k} = \sum_{k=0}^{\infty}\frac{t_{t+k}}{(1+h)^k} + \lim_{k\to\infty}\left[\frac{b_{t+k}}{(1+h)^k}\right] \tag{5}$$

This equation represents intertemporal budget balance: the government must plan to raise sufficient revenues to repay existing debt and finance planned expenditures. The last term is interesting for our argument. If time goes to infinity, this limit term should become equal to 0 (this is called the No-Ponzi condition). For finite cases, which are probably more interesting for our argument, this term may deviate from zero and represents the net wealth position of the government. Equation (5) tells us that if the government has debt outstanding, the present value of future primary deficits (g-t) must be positive, unless (in finite cases) the government is willing to reduce its net wealth.

What do we learn from this public accounting exercise?

1. Forward-looking agents will take this identity into account. In extreme form, consumers consider their holdings of government bonds equivalent to future tax obligations, leading to Ricardian equivalence (changes in tax policy only affect savings).
2. Projections of the real interest rate r and the GDP growth rate λ affect the "impact" of the value of current debt on future obligations. Since $h=r-\lambda$, all the terms in (5) point at this result. Projections that affect the GDP growth rate also affect the current value of future primary deficits.
3. Acknowledging period-to-period budget discipline does not guarantee intertemporal balance per se. Projections should take into account the desired net worth of the government sector.
4. Projections over a finite horizon have to be based on requirements with respect to government's net worth at the end of the horizon. Given argument 1, this probably affects the plans of agents.

5. Equation (5) is not only binding as such; the Maastricht treaty imposes alternative short-run restrictions, like *b* being less than 60 percent and *g-t* being smaller than 3 percent.

Now let us consider the examples given in *Keuzes in kaart 2003-2006*. Table 1.5 of the report illustrates the macroeconomic outcomes of the proposals of the various political parties. The budget surplus varies on average from 0.5 to 1.0 percent. What is the feedback of these findings? Does this imply that private savings grow faster in the 0.5% case? What are the consequences for net discounted government wealth? If the models had contained an equation like (5) these questions could have been answered straightaway.

Density forecasting

Most macroeconomic models present point forecasts; the CPB models are no exception. The way to present uncertainty, for instance with respect to changes in the exogenous variables, is to present outcomes of "high" and "low" scenarios. One can criticise this custom, although it definitely has attractive features. Point forecasts are easy to communicate by politicians and easy to understand for the general audience. How is uncertainty in the development of mean real wages according to eight political parties for twenty income categories in the years 2003-2006 to be reported?

Despite the advantage of simplicity, it is better to report more information with respect to the uncertainty of the outcomes. A second possibility to sketch uncertainty is to report prediction intervals. If one assumes a (symmetric, say Gaussian) distribution, one can employ a more detailed instrument: density forecasts. A density forecast of the realisation of a random variable at some future date of time is an estimate of the probability distribution of the possible future values of that variable (Tay and Wallis, 2000).

In the U.S. and the U.K. density forecasting has been practised for a long time. In the U.S. the ASA-NBER survey (or Survey of Professional Forecasters) is active since 1968. In the U.K. a Panel of Independent Forecasters was established in 1992. The members of the panels attach probabilities to given intervals for *e.g.* output growth and inflation. It is also possible to produce density forecasts with a macro-econometric model. For instance, in simple models past forecast errors can be used to measure the variance of a symmetric distribution around the point forecast. In large-scale non-linear systems, stochastic simulation methods are required. In these cases, asymmetrical distributions are more likely to be used.[8] It is also possible to present density functions for VAR Models.[9]

Table 3 contains an example for the 2002-2003 GDP growth rate in the U.S. It gives the mean probability 31 forecasters attach to possible changes in the GDP growth rate. One can see that the range of the forecasts is rather large, even for the intervals with higher densities.

Table 3 Density forecasts of US GDP-growth 2002-2003

GDP growth rate (%)	*Probability (%)*
6.0 or more	0.88
5.0 to 5.9	2.87
4.0 to 4.9	12.97
3.0 to 3.9	34.47
2.0 to 2.9	27.57
1.0 to 1.9	14.57
0.0 to 1.9	4.28
-1.0 to -0.1	4.28
-2.0 to -1.1	0.84
-2.0 or less	0.36

Source: Federal Reserve Bank of Philadelphia, Survey of Professional Forecasters, February 22, 2002 (http://www.phil.frb.org/files/spf/spfq102.pdf)

Figure 1 contains an illustration of an asymmetric density forecast: the rate of U.K. inflation (RPIX) as reported by the Bank of England panel. Here one can clearly observe that the distribution might have serious policy consequences, given the inflation target of 2.5%.

Figure 1 The February 2002 RPIX fan chart

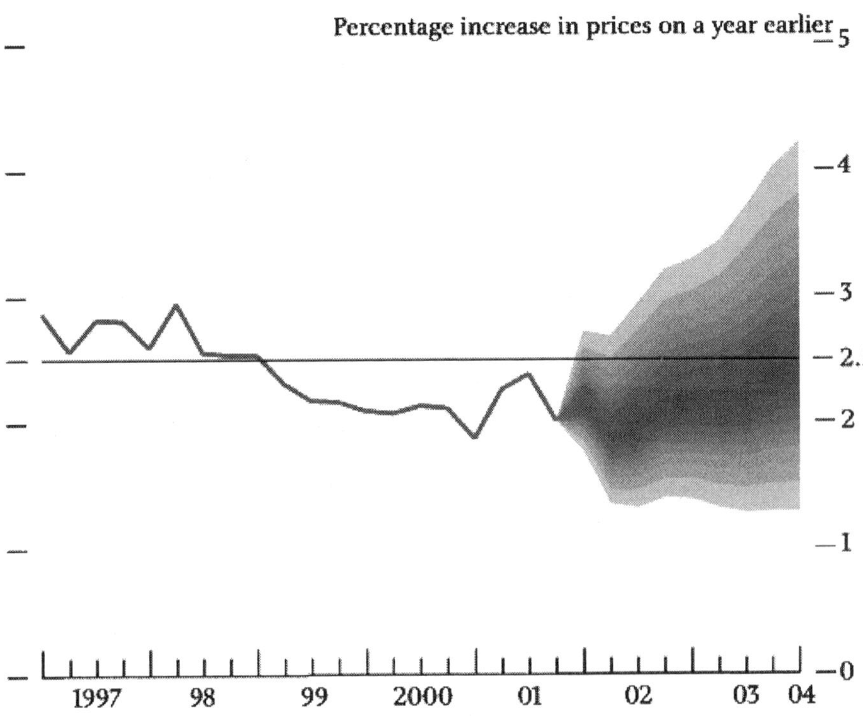

Source: Bank of England, Inflation report (http://www.bankofengland.co.uk/Links/setframe.html)

How can we apply these ideas to the CPB exercise? There is no trivial way, because uncertainty in forecasting is typically different from uncertainty in policy analysis. It is commonly assumed that forecasting uncertainty exceeds "policy" uncertainty. But policy analysis is based on the forecasting ability of the models used, so our "forecasting" uncertainty issues remain valid and valuable to discuss. Consider Table 1.6 in *Keuzes in Kaart 2003-2006* on the forecast of real wage increases. For single income earners the minimum real wage increase outcome varies from a minimum of 0.75% for GroenLinks to a maximum of 2% for the SP. If one calculates the density forecasts of the basis scenario of this experiment (no matter which method is used), these outcomes probably fit into the classes with high densities with large probability. In other words, the various policy scenarios are fully embedded in the forecasting uncertainty of the model.

5. CONCLUDING REMARKS

In this chapter, we sketch the international practise of macroeconomic modelling and the status of the CPB models. We conclude that, to a large extent, CPB meets international requirements. We believe that the CPB models are state-of-the-art instruments. CPB has a revealed preference for large-scale models and models based on econometric methodology (as compared to international competitors). This fact might be explained by the special institutional position of CPB as a government agency with tight networks to policy makers and data suppliers.[10] Although CPB does not have a formal monopoly in macro model building in the Netherlands, there is in fact only one domestic competitor. The Dutch Central Bank, *De Nederlandsche Bank,* operates the core models MORKMON for the Dutch economy and EUROMON for the European economy. In addition, there are two international competitors, the IMF and the OECD, although the latter copies CPB outcomes. High costs obstruct entrance to this market, since model development and maintenance is extremely costly and data and other information are sometimes not available to non-governmental institutions.

The models of CPB can be criticised. They lack forward-looking behaviour, treat the government sector as exogenous, and produce point forecasts only. For outsiders it is not fully clear how the model inputs are organised or how the models interact in policy analysis, which hampers the judgement of political parties' policy alternatives. We advocate more transparency of the models and model assumptions, the use of small-scale prototype forward-looking models, and density forecasts to represent uncertainty.

NOTES

* We thank Albert van der Horst (CPB) for useful suggestions.

1 See Hoogduin (1985).

2 See Wallis (2000).

3 See Clarida *et al.* (1999).

4 CPB (1997), or Huizinga (1998).

5 Gelauff and Graafland (1994), or Graafland and De Mooij (1998).

6 *Cf.* Church and Wallis (1998).
7 *Cf.* Graafland in this volume.
8 See Blake (1996).
9 See Kling and Bessler (1989).
10 See also Den Butter and Morgan (1998).

REFERENCES

Bank of England (1999), *Economic Models at the Bank of England*, London: Bank of England

Batini, N., and A.G. Haldane (1999), Forward-Looking Rules for Monetary Policy, in J.B. Taylor (Ed.), *Monetary Policy Rules*, Chicago: University of Chicago Press, 157-192

Blake, A.P. (1996), Forecast Error Bounds by Stochastic Simulation, *National Institute Economic Review*, 156, 72-79

Broer, D.P., R.A. de Mooij, and V.R. Okker (1998), CPB Models and their Uses, *CPB Report*, 98/3, 17-21

Butter, F.A.G. den, and M.S. Morgan (1998), What Makes the Models-Policy Interaction Successful?, *Economic Modelling*, 15(3), 443-475

Church, K.B., and K.F. Wallis (1998), Comment on JADE, *CPB Report*, 98/4, 49-50

Clarida, R., J. Galí, and M. Gertler (1999), The Science of Monetary Policy: A New Keynesian Perspective, *Journal of Economic Literature*, 37(4), 1661-1707

Cooley, T.F., and S.F. LeRoy (1985), Atheoretical Macroeconometrics: A Critique, *Journal of Monetary Economics*, 16(3), 83-308

CPB (1997), *JADE: A Model for the Joint Analysis of Dynamics and Equilibrium*, Working Paper 99, The Hague: CPB

CPB (1999), *WorldScan – The Core version*, The Hague: CPB

CPB (2002), *Keuzes in kaart 2003-2006. Economische effecten van acht verkiezingsprogramma's* ("Charting Choices 2003-2006. Economic Effects of Eight Election Programmes"), Den Haag: CPB

Darby, J., J. Ireland, C. Leith, and S. Wren Lewis (1999), COMPACT: A Rational Expectations, Intertemporal Model of the United Kingdom Economy, *Economic Modelling*, 16(1), 1-52

Donders, J., and H. Lunsing (1999), SAFE: A Model for Short-Term Analyses and Forecasts for the Dutch Economy, *CPB Report*, 99/3, 42-44

Fair, R.C. (1994), *Testing Macroeconometric Models*, Cambridge MA: Harvard University Press

Garratt, A., K. Lee, M.H. Pesaran, and Y. Shin (2002), A Long Run Structural Macroeconometric Model of the UK, *The Economic Journal*, forthcoming

Gelauff, G.M.M., and J.J. Graafland (1994), *Modelling Welfare State Reform,* Amsterdam: North-Holland

Graafland, J.J., and R.A. de Mooij (1998), MIMIC. An Appplied General Equilibrium Model for the Netherlands, *CPB Report*, 98/3, 27-31

Hargreaves, D. (1999), *SDS-FPS: A Small Demand-Side Version of the Forecasting and Policy System Core Model*, Reserve Bank of New Zealand Discussion Paper G99/10, Wellington: Reserve Bank of New Zealand

Heijdra, B.J., and F. van der Ploeg (2002), *Foundations of Modern Macroeconomics*, Oxford: Oxford University Press

Hoogduin, L.H. (1985), On the Character of Macroeconomics, Macroeconomic Policy and Econometrics: The Need for Another Macroeconomic Policy Conception, *Banca Nazionale del Lavoro Quarterly Review*, 164, 105-125

Huizinga, F. (1998), JADE. A Model for the Joint Analysis of Dynamics and Equilibrium, *CPB Report*, 98/3, 21-26

Jacobs, J.P.A.M. (1998), *Econometric Business Cycle Research*, Dordrecht/London: Kluwer Academic Publishers

Jacobs, J.P.A.M., and K.F. Wallis (2002), *Comparing SVARs and SEMs: More Shocking Stories*, Mimeo, Groningen: University of Groningen

Kling, J.L., and D.A. Bessler (1989), Calibration-Based Predictive Distributions: An Application of Prequential Analysis to Interest Rates, Money, Prices, and Output, *Journal of Business*, 62(4), 477-499

Kranendonk, H., and C. Jansen (1997), Using Leading Indicators in a Model-based Forecast, *CPB Report*, 97/3, 22-26

Lucas, R.E. (1976), Econometric Policy Evaluation: A Critique, in K. Brunner and A.H. Meltzer (Eds.), *The Phillips Curve and Labor Markets*, volume 1 of Carnegie-Rochester Conference Series, Amsterdam: North-Holland, 19-46

Mannaerts, H.J.B.M., M.G. Lijesen, and M. Mulder (2002), *ELMAR: A Model of the European Electricity Market*, CPB Discussion Paper (forthcoming)

McKibbin, W.J., and P.J. Wilcoxen (1999), The Theoretical and Empirical Structure of the G-Cubed Model, *Economic Modelling*, 16(1), 123-148

Pagan, A., and J. Robertson (2000), *Forecasting for Policy*, Mimeo, Canberra: Australian National University

RIVM (2002), *Verkiezingen 2002, Milieu & Natuur. Een beoordeling van de partijprogramma's van PvdA, D66, GroenLinks, ChristenUnie en SP* ("Elections 2002. Environment & Nature. An Assessment of the Party Programmes of PvdA, D66, GroenLinks, ChristenUnie and SP"), Bilthoven: RIVM

Tay, A.S., and K.F. Wallis (2000), Density Forecasting: A Survey, *Journal of Forecasting*, 19(4), 235-254

Vromans, M. (1998), ATHENA: The Multi-sector Model, *CPB Report*, 98/3, 32-36

Wallis, K.F. (2000), Macroeconometric Modelling, in M. Gudmundsson, T.T. Herbertsson, and G. Zoega (Eds.), *Macroeconomic Policy: Iceland in an Era of Global Integration*, Reykjavik: University of Iceland Press, 399-414

Wren-Lewis, S., J. Darby, J. Ireland, and O. Ricchi (1996), The Macroeconomic Effects of Fiscal Policy: Linking an Econometric Model with Theory, *The Economic Journal,* 106(436), 543-559

CHAPTER 6

JOHAN J. GRAAFLAND*

BALANCING INFORMATION AND UNCERTAINTY

1. INTRODUCTION

On 6 January 2001, Thaksin Shinawatra won the elections in Thailand by making many attractive promises without saying where all the money would come from. He pledged a three-year debt moratorium for perennially indebted farmers, along with a development fund of 1 million bath ($23,000) for each of Thailand's 70,000 villages. Some Bangkok-based analysts estimated that if Thaksin would honour all his promises, public debt would rise from 60% of GDP to as high as 100% of GDP. That would risk weakening the bath and could stoke the flames of inflation. As a result, the burden of Thaksin's populist pledges would boomerang straight back on the average Thais he promised to help (Crispin and Tasker, 2001).

In the Netherlands, Thaksin would probably not have been successful, because the political parties use to ask CPB Netherlands Bureau for Economic Policy Analysis (CPB) to analyse their electoral programmes and publish the results of this analysis just before the elections. The purpose of this procedure is to use the tools of economics to separate economic arguments from political preferences in a more or less neutral way. This raises the quality of the electoral programmes and clarifies the economic consequences of these programmes to the citizens. It brings home the need to combine tax cuts with unpopular reductions in public outlays, or alternatively, to finance attractive public expenditure with unpopular increases in the tax burden. Dependent on the political setting, the CPB report occasionally has had a significant impact on the political scene. For example, in 1998 the analysis of CPB showed that the Christian Democrat CDA's proposed policies would hardly reduce unemployment. This became a hotly debated topic and influenced the formation of the coalition after the elections. Afterwards, several economists voting on CDA doubted the quality of CPB's analysis.

Johan J. Graafland and Arie P. Ros (Eds.), Economic Assessment of Election Programmes: Does it Make Sense?, 61-79.

This raises the question of the likelihood of the outcomes published in the CPB report. Can we really be so confident in the tools of economics that we allow the CPB's report to have a major impact on the formation of the coalition for the next four years? How can we find a balance between using the information provided by economists without disregarding the uncertainty involved with this type of analysis? What does a proper balance imply for the presentation of the results?

In order to answer these questions, this chapter distinguishes between two types of analysis. Section 2 deals with the calculation of the *ex ante* budgetary consequences of the political programmes, where the degree of uncertainty is relatively low. Section 3 describes methodological aspects of several aspects of the analysis of overall *ex post* economic effects of the political programmes. Section 4 evaluates CPB as an audit institute of political parties by reviewing some procedural criteria. Section 5 summarizes the main conclusions.

2. CALCULATION OF THE *EX ANTE* BUDGETARY EFFECTS

The most attractive part of the CPB analysis of the election programmes of the political parties concerns the calculation of the *ex ante* budgetary effects of the proposals of the political parties in which behavioural consequences of the effects are not taken into account. In this case, the uncertainty in the numbers reported by CPB is relatively low, although not absent. For example, for the calculation of the budgetary effects of complex income tax reforms, a lot of information is needed about the number of people that belong to the groups that are affected, and sometimes this information is scarce or must be based on small samples of micro data.[1] Fortunately, CPB can sometimes check the calculations by comparing them with calculations of other agencies, like the Ministry of Finance, which owns a very detailed tax account for the Dutch population. This makes the calculation of the budgetary consequences a relatively easy task, whereas the impact on the quality of the political process is obvious. The political parties are forced to come up with consistent plans covering both the income and expenditures of the government and, during the process to formulating these plans, can learn from the CPB expertise.

Although the calculation of the *ex ante* budgetary effects of political programmes is informative, it only gives a partial insight into the full budgetary effects of these programmes. The policy measures will also generate behavioural effects that impact the government receipts and expenditures. Table 1, that reports the *ex ante* and *ex post* budgetary consequences of the political programmes in 1998, illustrates this. According to Table 1, the effectiveness of the various programmes differs significantly. For example, whereas the *ex ante* plans of the PvdA raise the budget deficit, *ex post* the budget deficit declines. This is due to a fall in government outlays caused by the wage reduction generated by the programme in combination with a rise in tax income caused by the positive impact of its programme on economic growth. In contrast, the behavioural effect of the Christian Democratic CDA programme is hardly favourable. *Ex post* the budget deficit declines only slightly more than in the *ex ante* plan. Focusing only on the *ex ante* budgetary consequences would therefore be ad hoc and lead to misjudgement of the various political programmes if these behavioural effects are substantial.

Table 1 Ex ante and ex post effects of political programmes on the government deficit[a]

	VVD	*PvdA*	*CDA*	*D66*	*Groenlinks*
Ex ante	-½	4	-3½	-¾	6½
Ex post	-5½	-1	-4½	-4½	4

[a] In billions of guilders. See Table III.1.2, III.2.2, III.3.2, III.4.2 and III.5.2 in CPB (1998). The *ex post* effects concern the impact on the government deficit in the fourth year after the implementation of the programme.

3. ESTIMATION OF THE *EX POST* OVERALL ECONOMIC IMPACT

A full analysis of these behavioural effects is also required to provide insight into the impact of these programmes on important economic goal variables, like the five traditional policy targets (full employment, price stability, a sound balance of payments, economic growth and a fair income distribution). Compared to the calculation of the *ex ante* budgetary effects of the political programmes, this is a relatively difficult task. Here the balance between the information content and the uncertainty of the analysis becomes more delicate. On the one hand, one can argue that any information is welcome. Indeed, since the CPB analysis affects the political strategy for the four coming years, any useful information and expertise that helps to raise the quality of the political choices is of high interest for the common good. On the other hand, because of this high interest, one should also be very careful when the outcomes of the analysis are highly uncertain. If policy measures are based on arguments for which the empirical base is absent or very weak, the probability that these measures do not solve the social problems, which they are intended to solve, is much higher.

The value of this type of analysis ultimately depends on the CPB models. Models are consequent and systematic metaphors that we employ for understanding aspects of the reality (Brümmer, 1993). For example, the behaviour of molecules can be explained by making a systematic comparison with the behaviour of billiard balls. In a similar way, economists try to understand the complexity of the modern economy by using large mathematical models that they know and understand. Although models help us understand the complex reality, economists are aware that every model is one-sided. There is a danger, however, that the development and systematic use of models diminish this awareness and create a conceptual blindness, especially if criticism on these models is scarce. In this respect, it is worrying that the attention of other economists for the large CPB models seems to decline. Whereas in the seventies economists from universities used to pay attention to the CPB models and criticized certain details of these models,[2] this attention has now shifted to other areas. Although CPB does a lot of effort to mobilize the criticism of other experts, economists at universities seldom scrutinise the details of these models, because this kind of analysis is useless for publications in top journals.

In order to calculate the *ex post* overall economic impact of the electoral proposals on important goals of economic policy, CPB uses a conglomerate of economic models, accounting schemes and qualitative analyses concerning the effects of changes in policy instruments that are not included in these models. For example, MIMIC is often used to analyse the long-term consequences of changes in the income tax and social security system that focus on the labour market, because of its detailed account of the income tax and the social security system. ATHENA is used for analysing the effects of measures that focus on the goods market, like environmental measures, because of its detailed description of the enterprise sector. The JADE model is used as an integrating framework to assess the medium and long-term overall effects of the political programmes.

There is, however, uncertainty how well the analysis provided by this method would mimic the real economic effects that will result from the electoral proposals. The uncertainty has (at least) five sources. The first three sources of uncertainty hold for the analysis with each of the models (JADE, MIMIC and ATHENA) used to analyse a subset of policy proposals and concern:

- the selection of economic mechanisms which are considered to be relevant for analysing these policy instruments,
- the selection of economic theories that describe the mechanisms,
- the empirical specification of the economic theories.

The last two types of uncertainty relate to the integration of information from different sources and concern:

- the integration of the results of different models,
- uncertainty following from the fact that some electoral proposals cannot be quantitatively analysed by CPB.

In this section we investigate these five sources of uncertainty.

Selection of economic mechanisms

If the set of policy instruments to be analysed by the model is determined, the researcher should select the most relevant economic mechanisms through which the policy instruments affect the economy. This means that the set of endogenous factors must be determined. Factors that are potentially relevant meet two conditions: first, they must be relatively sensitive to changes in the policy instruments to be analysed; second, they should exert a significant impact on important economic goals. If an economic factor is either hardly affected by the policy instrument (directly or indirectly) or hardly affects important goal variables itself, the economist may abstract from this factor or keep it exogenous.

Due to the limitation in research time and the increasing complexity, only the most relevant economic mechanisms can be endogenized. An additional complication is that it is difficult to determine from the beginning of the model construction which variables are relevant, because the (indirect) impact of policy instruments on endogenous variables and the impact of these endogenous variables on important goal variables can often only be calculated if the model is operational. Although it is often relatively easy to skip endogenous variables that appear to be irrelevant later on, it is in most cases much more complicated to endogenize exogenous variables in this stage. For example, the first operational version of

MIMIC (Gelauff and Graafland, 1994) was criticised because it did not model the impact of taxes on labour supply of breadwinners. The modelling of this mechanism required, however, a completely different model structure and it took more than one year to adapt the model accordingly. When the new version was operational, this effect indeed proved to be highly relevant.

A final remark with respect to the number of endogenous variables concerns the degree of disaggregation in the model. Although there are often *a priori* good reasons to assume that different types of households or different types of industries will be influenced in a different way, the mental limits of the model builder restrict the possibility to include too many distinctions. As the building and the use of the model is subject to a variety of errors, the reliability of the results must always be checked by the intuition of the model builder. If the total outcome of a simulation analysis is constructed as an aggregate of hundred substantial different outcomes, the model builder loses his intuitive grip on the model and is not able to detect errors made in the construction or use of the model. Another problem created by too much complexity is that it will be very difficult to communicate the results to outsiders. This especially holds if the model contains cross relations between variables at the lowest disaggregation level of different model blocks and if these relations are highly nonlinear.

Selection and specification of economic theory

After the selection of the set of policy instruments and endogenous variables, the researcher will have to consider the analytical tools for relating policy instruments and endogenous variables. For this purpose, proper economic theories have to be selected and, if necessary, adapted to the purpose of the model.

The method of developing economic theories is deductive. Usually, economists start with some core behavioural postulates, like the rationality of individuals (they have complete, transitive and continuous preferences, have perfect knowledge and have the cognitive ability to select the option they most prefer), consumerism (people are motivated by materialist acquisitiveness), methodological individualism (explanatory laws in economics concern features of individual human beings, *i.e.* agents independently optimise subject to constraints), and diminishing marginal rates of substitution. Combining these hypotheses with the restrictions that economic agents perceive (like budget and time constraints), the economists can derive analytically a theoretical relationship that relates endogenous variables to a set of explanatory variables, including policy instruments.[3] Having done only that, one has said nothing about the real world. Only if one believes that the behavioural postulates are true in reality, or at least can be regarded as a reasonable first approximation (or, alternatively, as inessential in the sense that the same implications would follow if more realistic assumptions would be used), the model can be applied to the real economy. However, as most economists recognize and experimental research more and more tends to confirm, the behavioural postulates depict a caricature of human behaviour. Still, theoretical economists are often reluctant to dethrone their core assumptions, because alternative (sociologically based) hypotheses are generally regarded as ad hoc and are only legitimate if they can be shown to follow from the standard generalizations about beliefs, preferences and constraints. This renders the results of economic models that rely heavily on this kind of postulates inexact in a deep sense.

Another reason for the inexactness of the economic theories follows from the limitation that the theory must be mathematically and conceptually tractable. As already noted before, too much complexity will reduce the economist's grip on the model and make communication of the results more difficult. This forces the economist to make many *ceteris paribus* clauses and simplifications.[4] Although the realism of the economic model can be improved by progressively adding complications and specific assumptions concerning the sort of phenomena to which the particular model will be applied, the room for this is limited. This considerably limits the scope for adding all kind of disturbing causes that in reality combine with the basic economic causes and explain the real economy. Since many of these other factors are not taken into account, the outcomes of the economic analysis only describe tendencies that are "true in the abstract" was it not for the disturbing causes.

Despite these humbling qualifications, economists are still very proud and secure about the relevance of their work. To quote Koopmans (1957):

> "The theories that have become dear to us can very well stand by themselves as an impressive and highly valuable system of deductive thought, erected on a few premises that seem to be well-chosen first approximations to a complicated reality ... to the extent one accepts their premises, their conclusions are highly relevant to questions of economic policy. In many cases the knowledge these deductions yield is the best we have ... comparable reasoning from premises recognized as more realistic has not been completed or has not yet been found possible."

Empirical basis of the model

Before economic theories can be applied to analyse concrete economic problems and derive policy implications, the theory should be confronted with the data. These economic data can be used to test alternative theories and to find behavioural parameters that provide the highest fit with the data.

When testing the realism of the economic theory, economists seldom consider the basic assumptions (Klant, 1982). All that is open to assessment are the sufficiency and accuracy of the other premises. Since economic phenomena are the effects of numerous causes, many of which the theory does not encompass, the correspondence between the data and the implications of theory is generally rather rough.

More problematic is that economists seem to be not very interested in testing their theories. Mark Blaug (1985) argues that economists rarely formulate their theories in ways that facilitate testing, carry out few tests and pay little attention to negative results. Why is testing so unimportant in economics? One reason might be that many economists are much more involved with non-empirical conceptual work. Another reason is the complexity of the economy. To test a theory requires knowledge of the subject and simple phenomena, so that few auxiliary assumptions are needed to derive predictions. Facing a complex and dynamic subject matter, economists cannot effectively test their theories. Hypotheses derived from economic theories can only be tested conditional on other untested hypotheses. As a result, the test results allow many interpretations without necessarily abandoning the core hypothesis. According to Klant (1982), this leaves the economist with a high degree of freedom and allows accepting a hypothesis on other grounds than on the basis of test results, including non-scientific beliefs. The feedback from empirical research on the formulation of hypotheses and theories is much weaker and the impact of cultural values correspondingly much larger in economic science than, for example, in natural sciences (Klant, 1987). A third reason is the lack of consistent databases. Especially in case of relatively new societal problems and instruments designed to solve these, a representative database, which is long enough to test alternative hypotheses, is often lacking. This problem is exacerbated by the fact that the social economic reality is much more likely to change rapidly in time than the natural processes. Universal numerical constants are lacking. A fourth reason is that experimental research is relatively more difficult for economics and the other social sciences compared to the natural sciences. Although experimental research is gaining interest and does help to test certain core hypotheses of economic theory, it remains uncertain how much the results obtained in the simplified experimental circumstances apply to actual economic life.

Instead of testing the core hypothesis of the underlying theories, most empirical work of CPB focuses on the estimates of behavioural parameters that are derived from underlying theories. Sometimes, as in the case of MIMIC, behavioural parameter values are taken from empirical research in the literature. These parameter values are surrounded with a confidence interval characterized by the standard deviation or t-value of the parameter. Although the estimate of the confidence interval of these behavioural parameters is also subject to uncertainty and depends, for example, on underlying untested assumptions (Don, 2001), these confidence intervals provide at least an opportunity to investigate the robustness of the analysis of the economic effects of the election programmes of the various political parties. In particular, one should like to perform a Monte Carlo analysis in order to estimate the possible range and probability of different outcomes implied by the confidence intervals of all behavioural parameters of the model. For CPB it is not possible to do this job within the limited time of three months in which the election programmes of eight parties must be analysed. Another problem is that some parameters are not based on empirical research or are taken from research derived from other theoretical models with a different structure. Finally, even if it would be possible to carry out such a Monte Carlo analysis, it might be difficult to interpret the results. However, a clear interpretation is both necessary for preventing errors in the process of calculating the effects and for communicating the results to the political parties.

A less demanding method to illustrate the uncertainty of the results is by performing sensitivity analysis with a subset of parameter values. Although this method does not provide a full estimate of the probability of certain outcomes, it generates some insight into their robustness. Recently, CPB has developed a systematic method to perform sensitivity analysis with MIMIC. In particular, Graafland *et al.* (2001) present some sensitivity analysis on the electoral proposals of three political parties in 1998. Some outcomes for the (conservative) liberal VVD and the social democrat PvdA are presented in Table 2.

Table 2 Sensitivity analyses of the projected labour market effects of the tax proposals of VVD and PvdA in 1998, according to MIMIC

	Employment growth		*Fall in unemployment rate*	
	VVD	PvdA	VVD	PvdA
Base version MIMIC	2.5	2.3	- 0.7	- 0.8
Lower wage elasticity of labour supply	2.4	1.8	- 0.7	- 0.8
Lower export elasticity	2.1	1.8	- 0.5	- 0.6
No real wage resistance	1.7	1.3	- 0.2	- 0.2

Source: Graafland *et al.* (2001), Table 14.5.

As is shown in Table 2, the labour market effects of the tax proposals of VVD and PvdA change substantially if the parameter values are varied, but the relative ranking does not alter. In the first sensitivity analysis (second row in Table 2), the wage elasticity of labour supply by partners of breadwinners is reduced from 1.0 to 0.5. In the empirical literature these estimates vary from about 0.4 to 1.2.[5] As a result, the tax proposal of the PvdA becomes less effective because its tax reduction is targeted on partners. In the third row, the partial elasticity of substitution between domestic and foreign goods and services is reduced from 3.0 to 1.25 (which can be regarded as the lowest value found by empirical research). In this case, the effectiveness of both the VVD and the PvdA tax proposal is reduced by about 25%, but, again, the relative effectiveness does not change. In the last row, the impact of the tax wedge on wages is adapted from 0.44 to 0.00. Whereas empirical evidence for the Netherlands usually confirms the presence of this so-called real wage resistance (although not very significant), international literature puts doubts on its existence for many other countries. Another reason to doubt the magnitude of this real wage resistance effect in 1998 was the relatively tight labour market situation in this period, which reduces the probability that the tax reduction proposed by the VVD and the PvdA would induce wage moderation. If real wage resistance is absent, the MIMIC calculations show that the effects of the electoral programmes on unemployment are much smaller.

Empirical validation is not only necessary for the assessment of behavioural parameters, these data are also necessary for providing the base path of the model that determines the magnitude of the phenomena to which policy instruments relate. Although these data are relatively easy to obtain, databases underlying highly disaggregated models like MIMIC are also subject to uncertainty. This is partly due to the fact that these data are constructed on the bases of different and often inconsistent underlying databases. Therefore, additional assumptions have to be made to construct a consistent database that fits the model structure. Another complication concerns the end year of the simulation designed to analyse the consequences of the policy measures (which is 2012 in the case of MIMIC). For this projection period, assumptions have to be made with respect to the base path of the model. Since the simulation results depend critically on the level of certain economic variables, this creates an additional uncertainty with respect to the effectiveness of these policy instruments. For example, in MIMIC the effectiveness of policy measures designed to reduce unemployment depends very much on the level of unemployment in the end year of the base path.[6]

Integrating the information of different models

The economic models used by CPB are relatively large. The advantage of using large models is that they allow studying the effects of a broad range of policy measures with one model. This improves the consistency and comparability of the results of the economic analysis of the various policy proposals.

Still, for the analysis of the election programmes, one CPB model will not suffice. In order to include the detailed information that is necessary to discriminate between the economic effects of different details of the many policy proposals, CPB needs different models for different purposes. Using one model that would capture all these details and the dynamic structure to project the effects of these proposals over time would render a huge and completely intractable and incomprehensible economic model. As a result, the model builder will loose his intuitive grip on the model and his ability to detect errors made in the construction and use of the model. Such a model would turn into a black box to the model builders themselves and make any outcome highly unreliable and therefore useless.

For this reason, CPB uses at least three large economic models.[7] MIMIC is used to analyse the long-term consequences of changes in the income tax and social security system that focus on the labour market. ATHENA is used for analysing the effects of measures that focus on particular economic sectors, like environmental measures. The JADE model is used as an integrating framework to assess the medium and long-term overall effects of the political programmes. Since these models have not been set up as one consistent modular system, in which detailed model blocks can be switched on respectively switched off, the use of these three models introduces problems of consistency and comparability. This is illustrated by Table 3, which reports the calculated long-term labour market effects of the election programmes in 1998 of the VVD and the PvdA respectively by MIMIC and JADE.[8]

Table 3 The projected labour market effects of the VVD and PvdA election programme in 1998, according to MIMIC and JADE

		VVD	*PvdA*
Employment growth market sector	MIMIC	2.2	2.4
	JADE	2.0	1.6
Reduction in unemployment rate	MIMIC	- 0.8	- 1.3
	JADE	- 1.3	- 0.6

Table 3 shows that the employment effects projected by MIMIC and JADE substantially differ. According to MIMIC, the PvdA is more successful than the VVD in stimulating employment growth, whereas JADE finds an opposite result. The underlying determinants of the employment growth also differ. In MIMIC, the employment growth of the VVD programme goes together with (and is largely caused by) a substantial increase in labour supply and a rather modest fall in unemployment. In contrast, JADE projects almost no labour supply effects of the VVD programme and a relatively large reduction in unemployment. As a result, in case of the unemployment effect, the ranking of the VVD and PvdA programmes is reversed.

More generally, the results of Table 3 once again illustrate the uncertainty involved with economic analysis. Although the JADE and MIMIC model are based on the same empirical research as much as possible (in order to prevent this kind of divergences), these models can still yield very different results for complex packages of policy proposals, because of differences in the more specific details of the models. It should be noted, however, that there are potentially two reasons that explain the difference in outcomes. First, the set of measures analysed by MIMIC is not exactly the same as the set of measures analysed by JADE. However, since the divergence in inputs that determine equilibrium unemployment (replacement ratio and reduction in collective burden) is rather small, this cannot explain the difference in results. Second, we should acknowledge that the realisation of the equilibrium described by MIMIC might take more than the eight years reported for JADE. However, still one would at least expect a tendency towards similar results. Since MIMIC lacks a dynamic structure, we do not exactly know the speed of the structural supply effects described by this model and how much JADE should be corrected for specific results obtained by MIMIC. This is just another uncertainty in the analysis.

Probably, the difference in outcomes will even be larger if two or more economic independent institutes would analyse the electoral programmes. An illustration is Van Bergeijk and Haffner (1994), who analysed the effects of the electoral proposals in 1994 with INERT (an applied general equilibrium model developed by the Ministry of Economic Affairs). For three political parties their analysis yields rather similar outcomes as CPB (1994), but for the PvdA and GroenLinks the difference is very large. According to INERT, the predicted annual GDP growth for the PvdA is equal to 0.7%, against 1.9% reported in CPB (1994), whereas for GroenLinks even the sign was reversed: instead of 1.5% they found –0.3%. Similar differences were obtained for employment growth.

The integration of quantitative and qualitative information and the role of additional assumptions

The economic CPB models must not only meet scientific criteria of sound research, they must also be relevant in light of the actual policy questions. Fitting economic models to all major actual policy questions is a hard job, because the construction of an applied economic model takes considerable time (varying from at least two years to about five years). It is not possible to foresee all policy questions and instruments that will be relevant in the election time. Even if most of the policy instruments that will be proposed in the election programmes would be foreseeable, there are two other restrictions on the number of policy instruments included in the model. First, as the analysis of the economic impact of a certain policy instrument often takes a considerable time, the limited time available for research poses restrictions on the number of policy instruments. A second restriction is that the model must maintain a clear and verifiable structure. If too many policy instruments and economic mechanisms through which they affect the economy are included, the users of the model will loose their grip on the model and, consequently, the model will become untransparent which strongly diminishes its reliability.

Policy proposals that relate to policy instruments for which an economic analysis is not available yet must therefore be dealt with in a less thorough way. This implies that the uncertainty of the CPB analysis increases with the number of unconventional policy instruments. This number will be related to various factors, like the number of new political parties that ask CPB to analyse their programme and the number of societal issues that are relatively new and ask for innovative policy instruments. How to include this kind of proposals in the overall estimate of the effects of the electoral programmes?

In these cases, CPB faces three alternatives. First, if an empirical estimate of these proposals is very difficult, it is possible to use theoretical notions in combination with *ex ante* statistical information to give a qualitative description of the expected effectiveness of the proposals without presenting numbers based on a quantitative model. The advantage of this method is that it provides relevant information about the possible effects involved with the policy proposals without unwarranted pretension about the quantitative impact of these measures. Such a systematic qualitative analysis of the pros and cons of a concrete policy proposal generates at least an idea of the possible risks involved. The disadvantage of this method is that additional qualitative notions in the CPB report of the analysis of election programmes are in most cases hardly noticed in the media and therefore tend to be neglected in the elections and policy process later on.

Another possibility of integrating qualitative insights into the quantitative analysis is by making crude quantitative assumptions about the expected impact of these proposals. This strategy is especially relevant if the qualitative analysis suggests that the policy proposal has an unambiguous and strong impact on the economy. Refraining from quantification might be more harmful than using a highly uncertain assumption to quantify the effect and, by doing so, integrate the effect of the policy proposal in the overall analysis to be presented in the media. The disadvantage of this method is, however, that if CPB presents total effects of the policy proposals, the relatively certain effects of policy proposals for which CPB has proper instruments is combined with relatively uncertain effects derived from crude additional assumptions. How should we value a very favourable but also highly uncertain effect of the programme of political party A in comparison to a more modest but also more certain favourable effect of the programme of political party B? Without discounting the degree of uncertainty, CPB will add up apples and pears.[9]

A third alternative is that CPB highlights the uncertainty by making several alternative assumptions about the possible effect of the policy measure and investigating the range of outcomes. This would increase the insight into the risks involved with the policy measure, but still allow integration into the quantitative CPB analysis of the other proposals. The disadvantage of this approach is that it might be impossible to quantify the probabilities of alternative assumptions. Another danger is that the analysis becomes so complicated that the readers of the CPB report will fail to interpret the results properly. For example, when ranges of outcomes replace point estimates, it will become much more difficult to describe the trade-offs between various electoral programmes, because these trade-offs may qualitatively differ for different outcomes.

Finally, there is one other point of concern with respect to the role of assumptions. As Klant (1987) argues, the lack of objective empirical information implies that subjective notions affect the weighting of arguments in an economic analysis. This especially holds for those parts of the analysis with the weakest empirical base. This implies that the general way how economists perceive the world, society and history will affect their economic analysis and conclusions. Since economists at CPB have their own professional background and, in general, little practical experience with several aspects of the real economy, like business, unemployment, *et cetera*, it is likely that their opinions and assumptions differ from the perceptions of other people like businessmen or social workers. A recent example of such a conflict is the debate between CPB and representatives of the employers' and labour organisations about the effectiveness of the proposal of the Social Economic Council to combat the high rate of disability in the Netherlands. One of the arguments of the Social Economic Council was that the agreement and commitment of employers' and labour organisations to this plan would be one of the crucial factors guaranteeing its success. This is a type of argument that is not in the CPB analysis. Nor do CPB economists feel that they should make additional assumptions to include such a "consensus and commitment effect".

4. DOES CPB MEET PROCEDURAL CRITERIA OF AN AUDIT INSTITUTE?

During election time, CPB operates as an independent audit institute of the political parties. In the literature of business ethics, several procedural criteria have been developed for such audit processes. It is interesting to view the role of CPB in this perspective. Just as audit bureaus have to control business units for compliance with the code of conduct, CPB has to review the programmes of political parties in order to see whether they hold the norm that you should not deceive the voter by presenting partial plans that do not present the real cost in the longer run. Just as in business, political parties are not forced to undergo this audit process, but voluntarily choose for this option in order to convince the public of the high quality of their election programme. But once they agree to be audited, they should remain committed to it. A political party that starts the process but seeks to withdraw halfway, will loose its credibility anyway.

In order to evaluate the role of CPB as an audit institute, we use several criteria. Kaptein (1998) and Zadek, Prudan and Evans (1997) develop several norms. Table 4 summarizes these standards and applies them to the audit of the political parties.[10]

Table 4 Procedural evaluation of the analysis of the electoral political programmes

Norm	*Application*
Completeness and evolution	All *ex ante* budgetary consequences are analysed, but only the quantifiable *ex post* economic consequences are included in the assessment.
Transparency	CPB publishes a public report, but the *ex post* economic results cannot be replicated by other scientists.
Independency	CPB is independent, but the *ex post* economic results depend on the general perceptions of CPB's workers.
Consistency and comparability	CPB uses several models to evaluate the programmes of different parties and auxiliary assumptions are made to integrate the results of these models.
Supportability, clarity, stakeholder participation and achievability	CPB assists all political parties by making suggestions during the audit. Political parties can bring in information and influence the judgement of CPB, but political parties in the government have more opportunities to do this. The supply of highly concrete proposals is not achievable for many parties.
Management systems and continuous improvement	CPB has a well-organised database to evaluate the budgetary effects, and is constantly improving its instruments used for executing the audit. However, because of the high workload, a thorough and systematic study of the economic consequences of new topics is not possible.

Completeness and evolution

CPB requires that the political parties give a complete overview of all plans that generate effects on the public budget in order to assess the budgetary consequences. Although CPB does not require from the political parties a full intertemporal account that closes the government budget in the longer run, it summarizes this information by calculating the overall impact of the programmes on the government deficit. The completeness of the analysis of *ex post* economic effects of the electoral proposals is, however, more limited. Innovative policy proposals for which CPB lacks proper instruments cannot be taken into account in the quantitative judgement of the overall impact on the government budget and other important goals of economic policy.

With respect to the criterion of evolution, it is also more difficult to control whether political parties really intend to execute the measures they communicate to CPB. Indeed, sometimes political parties adapt the details of their plans with the sole purpose to generate attractive figures in the CPB report without explicit democratic discussion of these changes, nor intending to implement the measures when the party would participate in the government coalition. Although CPB tends to refuse avaricious plans, it must also respect the freedom of the representatives of the political parties. This leaves them some room to supply input for the CPB analysis which probably lacks a strong political consent from the party.

Transparency

Transparency is a common norm to scientific research. According to Merton (1968), the ethos of institutionalised science consists of four norms: communism, universalism, disinterestedness and organized scepticism. The first norm, communism, refers to the common ownership of goods and is very much related to transparency. The fruits of science belong to community. Applying this to the analysis of electoral proposals means that other scientists can replicate the results.[11] This requires that other economists of economic bureaus should have access to the tools used and should be informed how the results are derived. Although CPB regularly publishes detailed descriptions of the models used for analysing the election programmes, the actual translation of policy proposals into input for these models and the way the results of these models are integrated in the report remain a black box. This especially holds for the analysis of the *ex post* economic consequences. The analysis is too complex and the time for carrying out the analysis too short to document the process and the reasons behind the many choices that have to be made in order to arrive at a coherent and plausible story of the economic effects of the various political programmes.

Independency

Independency is also a standard norm to scientific research and related to the other norms mentioned by Merton: universalism, disinterestedness and organized scepticism. Universalism reflects that knowledge claims are to be assessed by impersonal criteria precluding particularism. Disinterestedness means that the scientist is to pursue the quest for knowledge in a disinterested way. No matter whether the scientist is motivated by scientific curiosity or personal gain, never is (s)he allowed to let personal interests interfere with the quest for truth as such. Finally, organized scepticism is connected to a critical and careful questioning of the research question. Nothing is to be excluded from close scrutiny (De Laat, 2001). Independency is also explicitly mentioned in the mission statement of CPB, which states that its mission is to provide independent forecasts and analyses that are scientifically sound and relevant for policy makers. Independency is required because the CPB analysis of the election programmes should be done in an objective way. Since the political parties do not have to pay for the study, CPB is not financially dependent of them. Furthermore, independency also requires that the personal political conviction of the researchers should not affect the analysis. There is no reason to believe that CPB does not meet this criterion. Personally, I believe that the CPB economists are very upright. This is also illustrated by the fact that in the past, confidential information has never come out in the media before publication of the CPB report. The only point of concern is that, due to the lack of scientific transparency in combination with the room for subjective judgements, the general way how CPB economists perceive the world, society and history, will affect their economic analysis and conclusions.

Consistency and comparability

According to Klant (1987), the power of economic analysis lies in its consistency rather than in the accuracy of the outcomes of the analysis. Using only one audit institute improves the consistency and comparability of the analysis of the electoral programmes. Compared to other institutes, in terms of manpower and analytical tools available, CPB seems to be the most qualified institute to perform this job. Still, because of the complexity of the analysis, it is impossible for CPB to provide a fully (theoretical) consistent analysis. Since CPB uses different tools for different proposals and since the set of proposals differs for each political party, the mixture of tools and models used to analyse these electoral programmes also differs for each political party. In order to calculate the total impact of each programme on important goals of economic policy, auxiliary assumptions must be made that differ for each party.

Still, one can argue that the consistency and comparability is best secured by appointing only one institute with this task. If more institutes were involved, the consistency and comparability would further diminish as each institute would use its own instruments and make different auxiliary assumptions to assess the overall impact of the electoral programmes. This is particularly true if the political parties will select only one institute for analysing their programme. In that case, political parties might shop for the most attractive results.

One can wonder, however, whether some competition between different institutes has also some advantages, provided that the institutes involved consider a similar set of electoral programmes. With respect to the *ex ante* budgetary consequences, one would expect similar outcomes because of the lower degree of uncertainty involved in this part of the analysis. More divergence will be obtained in the analysis of the *ex post* economic consequences. But one could argue that the variance in results of different institutes is also informative, because it informs the public about the high degree of uncertainty that underlies this type of analysis.

In the most recent election, three political parties (CDA, SP and LN) actually asked NYFER, a private Economic Bureau at the University of Nyenrode, to analyse the economic effects of their programmes. Unfortunately, NYFER refused by arguing that such an analysis is only useful if these parties would come up with significantly distinguishing proposals, which is not the case according to its director at that time Eduard Bomhoff.[12] Another reason might be that the government does not subsidize alternative analyses, whereas CPB, which is fully funded by the government, does offer this service for free.

Supportability, clarity, stakeholder participation and achievability

CPB also supports the political parties by making suggestions. Indeed, since the criteria implicit in the tools used by CPB are highly complex, political parties are often unaware of the crucial factors that determine the CPB judgement. The clarity of the audit process is therefore relatively weak. In order to raise the clarity, the political parties are also informed during the audit process about the possible consequences of their programmes and allowed to make final adaptations before publication of the results.

Still, one can wonder whether the competition between all political parties is fair in all respects. In particular, it is a public secret that the political parties who are in office during election time make more use of the expertise that is present in the ministries. Although CPB cannot be blamed for this situation, the advantages of this position are enhanced by the CPB analysis, because the officials of the ministries are relatively well-known with the instruments and analysis of CPB. On the other hand, if CPB would not perform this analysis, the political parties who are in government during election time would also benefit from their position because of the better access to information in the ministries. On balance, CPB therefore probably contributes to an equal access of political parties to public information.

Another point of concern is whether the criteria set by CPB are feasible for the political parties, as CPB requires very detailed information. Can one really expect from the political parties that they are able to work out all the details of their electoral programmes that are normally worked out by specialized officials of the government? There is a danger that this focus on economic details will diminish the attention to the broader political aspects of the electoral programmes.

Management systems and continuous improvement

CPB has a well-organised database to calculate the budgetary consequences of the political parties, and a good network of relations with other institutes, including the Central Bureau of Statistics and the Ministry of Finance to check its calculations or demand additional information. Since CPB has a long experience with the analysis of election programmes of political parties, it has also developed systematic procedures to improve the instruments required for this analysis, including planning schemes that take care that these instruments are operational when the analysis must be done.

Still, despite this long experience, the analysis of (currently) eight electoral programmes each containing many proposals is a huge task, whereas the time for performing this analysis is relatively short (about three months). This creates a high workload and leaves little room for additional research on new topics.

5. CONCLUSIONS

This chapter reviews the uncertainty involved with different aspects of the CPB analysis of the electoral programmes of the political parties in the Netherlands. The more uncertain, the less informative and useful this analysis is.

In section 2, I conclude that the uncertainty involved in the analysis of the *ex ante* budgetary consequences of the electoral proposals is relatively small. For this aspect, the CPB analysis is highly informative and useful. It prevents political parties to come up with popular electoral proposals without presenting the costs in terms of a rise in budget deficit and public debt in the future. Therefore, as far as the *ex ante* budgetary consequences are concerned, CPB operates very well as an audit institute of the political parties.

Section 3 casts doubt whether the balance between information and uncertainty is also as favourable for the analysis of the *ex post* economic effects of the political programmes. The main reason is that the economic effects of the electoral programmes are highly complex, whereas the tools that economic science offers are subject to a high degree of uncertainty. In the process of the construction of the tools to investigate the economic consequences of the electoral proposals, many choices and abstractions must be made to arrive at a point estimate of the overall economic effects of the various electoral programmes. Because of this uncertainty, a presentation of point estimates of the overall effects of the electoral programmes on important goals of economic policy might therefore mislead rather than inform the public. Keuzenkamp (2001) even argues that the scientific illusion of the large CPB models may be harmful to the profession of economics.

This does not imply that an analysis of the *ex post* economic effects is not useful or should remain in abeyance, but that the ambition of this analysis should be more modest. Instead of only presenting point estimates of the overall economic effects of various political parties, CPB should also illustrate the uncertainty by a Monte Carlo analysis or a sensitivity analysis with some well-chosen alternatives. Although this might further complicate the analysis and the communication of the results, the advantage would be that the political parties and the public will be more able to form their opinion on the uncertainty associated with the CPB analysis. For this purpose, a Monte Carlo analysis with a small transparent model that illustrates the main mechanisms might be a first step. Such an analysis might show that there is a range of defendable rankings of the effectiveness of the various electoral programmes of the political parties. Besides making uncertainty more explicit, the sensitivity analysis should also indicate whether there are major risks with respect to the realisation of important policy goals.

NOTES

* The author thanks Henk Don and Lans Bovenberg for their comments on an earlier version of this chapter.

1 Take for example the introduction of an optional joint income tax system for households consisting of a breadwinner and a partner, in which these households can prefer the option of summing up the income of breadwinner and partner and splitting it into two equal parts before applying the tax code. Calculation of the budgetary consequences requires for all households information about the gross income of both breadwinner and partner per household to determine how many households will choose for this option and what the implied tax reduction will be.

2 *E.g.* Driehuis and Van der Zwan (1978).

3 For a critique, see Simon (1979), Sen (1987), Hausman (1992), Conlisk (1996), Rabin (1998) and Van Liedekerke (2000).

4 Hausman (1992) argues that a statement with a *ceteris paribus* clause is defendable if four conditions are met: the statement must be law-like; the *ceteris paribus* law must be reliable; the law is refinable in the sense that if specific qualifications are added, the law becomes more reliable; the statement is excusable in the sense that disturbing causes must be identified.

5 See Table 4.1 in Graafland *et al.* (2001).

6 Although the policy analysis is more linear for JADE and ATHENA and therefore less sensitive to the baseline path of these models, this is hardly an advantage, since this simplification does not

reduce but only abstracts from the uncertainty following from the nonlinear character of real economic relationships.

7 See also the chapter by Don in this volume.

8 For MIMIC, we use the combined results of the third respectively fourth column of Table II.1.1 and II.1.3 of CPB (1998). For JADE the results are taken from the fourth column of Table III.3.1 respectively Table III.1.1 of CPB (1998) which reflect the impact after eight years.

9 This lack of comparability also holds if the time horizon of the major effects of the various electoral programmes varies significantly. As CPB (2002) only reports the macroeconomic effects in the medium term, the long-term effects do not become visible.

10 Another criterion is the sanctionability. This criterion is secured, because the political parties that do not submit their programme to CPB or do not rank high according to the criteria of CPB, risk a loss in reputation. See the chapter by Van der Lecq in this volume.

11 Also Kleijnen (2000) argues that replication is a basic principle of science. He pleas that the users of models should present the readers with a set of non-dominated solutions. Depending on the reader's values, they decide.

12 See NRC of 25 March 2002.

REFERENCES

Bergeijk, P.A.G. van, and R.C.G. Haffner (1994), The Economic Consequences of Dutch Politics, *De Economist*, 142(4), 497-505

Blaug, M. (1985), Comment on D. Wade Hand's "Karl Popper and Economic Methodology: A New Look", *Economics and Philosophy*, 1(2), 286-289

Brümmer, V. (1993), *Liefde van God en mens* ("Love of God and Man"), Kampen: Kok Agora

Conlisk, J. (1996), Why Bounded Rationality?, *Journal of Economic Literature*, 34(2), 669-700

CPB (1994), *Vijf verkiezingsprogramma's. Economische gevolgen van voorgenomen beleid*, ("Five Election Programmes. Economic Effects of Proposed Policies") The Hague: Sdu Uitgeverij

CPB (1998), *Keuzes in kaart. Economische effecten van vijf verkiezingsprogramma's* ("Charting Choices. Economic Effects of Five Election Programmes"), The Hague: Sdu Uitgeverij

CPB (2002), *Keuzes in kaart. Economische effecten van acht verkiezingsprogramma's*, ("Charting Choices. Economic Effects of Eight Election Programmes"), The Hague: Sdu Uitgeverij

Crispin, S.W., and R. Tasker (2001), Thailand Incorporated, *Far Eastern Economic Review*, 164(2), 16-18

Don, F.J.H. (2001), Forecasting in Macroeconomics: A Practitioner's View, *De Economist*, 149(2), 155-175

Driehuis, W., and A. van der Zwan (Eds.) (1978), *De voorbereiding van het economisch beleid kritisch bezien* ("A Critical Look at Policy Design"), Leiden: Stenfert Kroese

Gelauff, G.M.M., and J.J. Graafland (1994), *Modelling Welfare State Reform*, Amsterdam *et cetera*: North-Holland

Graafland, J.J, R.A. de Mooy, A.G.H. Nibbelink, and A. Nieuwenhuis (2001), *MIMICing Tax Policies and the Labour Market*, Amsterdam *et cetera*: North-Holland

Hausman, D.M. (1992), *The Inexact and Separate Science of Economics*, Cambridge U.K.: Cambridge University Press

Kaptein, M. (1998), *Ethics Management: Auditing and Developing the Ethics Content of Organisations*, Dordrecht: Kluwer Academic Publishers

Keuzenkamp, H.A. (2001), *Wat zijn economen waard?* ("What Are Economists Worth?"), Inaugural lecture, Amsterdam: Vossiuspers UvA

Klant, J.J. (1982), Idealisatie: idee en ideaal ("Idealization: Idea and Ideal"), in B. de Gaay Fortman (Ed.), *Economie en waarde*, ("Economics and Value"), Jaarboek Studiekring Post-Keynesiaanse economie, Alphen aan den Rijn: Samsom, 9-47

Klant, J.J. (1987), *Filosofie van de economische wetenschappen*, ("Philosophy of Economic Science"), Leiden: Martinus Nijhoff

Kleijnen, J.P.C. (2000), Ethical Issues in Modeling: Some Reflections, *European Journal of Operational Research*, 130(1), 223-230

Koopmans, T.C. (1957), *Three Essays on the State of Economic Science*, New York: McGraw-Hill

Laat, P.B. de (2001), Open Source Software: A New Mertonian Ethos?, in A. Vedder (Ed.), *Ethics and the Internet*, Antwerpen/Groningen/Oxford: Intersentia, 33-47

Liedekerke, L. van (2000), *Values in Economy and Economics*, Ph.D. Dissertation, Leuven: Katholieke Universiteit Leuven

Merton, R.K. (1968), Science and Democratic Social Structure, in R.K. Merton, *Social Theory and Social Structure*, Enlarged Ed., New York/London: Free Press, 604-615

Rabin, M. (1998), Psychology and Economics, *Journal of Economic Literature*, 36(1), 11-46

Sen, A. (1987), *On Ethics and Economics*, Oxford *et cetera*: Blackwell

Simon, H. A. (1979), Rational Decision Making in Business Organisations, *The American Economic Review*, 69(4), 493-513

Zadek, S., P. Prudan, and R. Evans (1997), *Building Corporate Accountability*, London: Eartscan Publications

PART III

POLITICAL ASPECTS

CHAPTER 7

S.G. (FIEKE) VAN DER LECQ

CALCULATED CHOICES: WHO PROFITS?

1. INTRODUCTION

In the Netherlands, government elections have a unique feature: the election programmes of the (larger) parties are assessed for their economic impact by the independent CPB Netherlands Bureau for Economic Policy Analysis (CPB). This bureau was founded by Jan Tinbergen, with the explicit aim to increase the understanding of the workings of the economy without any inference of political norms.[1] By building models to calculate such workings, the insight was gained and became increasingly used for underpinning the Dutch governmental policy actions.

Since the nineteen-eighties, political parties have found their way to CPB. About half a year in advance of the elections, once the election programmes of the parties are developed, the parties consult CPB. In close collaboration between the parties' economic representatives and the CPB researchers, the programmes are translated into parameter values which are used to calculate the economic outcomes of the election programmes. This process has its advantages and disadvantages, as will be discussed below.

The fact that the impact calculation does take place, is for two reasons not sufficient to conclude that the pros are larger than the cons. First, it is possible that the by now traditional calculation procedure is a case of path dependency, a habitual procedure which happens to have evolved in history, with a suboptimal result. It can be a conventional thing to do, like a ceremony, without enough welfare gains of its own. Concluding that an act is welfare increasing from the simple fact that it is done is *ex post* rationalisation and the easy way out. It hinges upon assumptions regarding rationality, information, foresight and transaction costs. The government, political parties and the voters are not likely to all satisfy these assumptions. Second, even if the calculation improves welfare, the question as to who gains and who pays deserves attention. As long as redistribution is not without costs, if possible at all, someone's pros may be another one's cons. This holds in particular for the voter

Johan J. Graafland and Arie P. Ros (Eds.), Economic Assessment of Election Programmes: Does it Make Sense?, 83-95.

who pays the tax money which is used to do the calculations. Does the voter profit and how does (s)he perceive the gain?

Also the extent of the impact calculation project deserves analysis. Over time, more parties joined the project by demanding an evaluation of their election programme. Also, the scope of the impact calculation was broadened, so that the CPB effort increased substantially.[2] It remains unclear whether a cost-benefit analysis is made and by whom. After all, CPB is paid for anyway, so the decision to put more or less effort in the impact calculation project is part of the CPB planning cycle. By implication, the effort on behalf of the impact calculation will be traded off against other CPB projects and regular activities. An integral welfare analysis of the impact calculation, including a sensitivity analysis with respect to budget and effort, is not (publicly) available.

The analysis starts from scratch by raising the issue as to how and why the procedure could have come into existence if no historical peculiarities or path dependency existed. Does an information problem exist, who has the problem and what are the logical ways to solve it? After having identified the incentives to have election programmes calculated and the figures revealed, the fact that CPB does perform the calculations is taken as given, and the impact on the preparation of the elections is analysed. In order to assess the impact of the extra information on the voting process, this chapter then focuses on the voter. Then, the question can be answered as to who profits from the impact calculations, and who pays for it.

2. THE INFORMATION PROBLEM

Suppose the Netherlands do not have the traditional CPB impact calculations. Then, the political parties will present their election programmes to the voters, with or without any statement regarding the economic consequences of the proposed policy actions. Maybe the parties themselves do not even know the economic impact of their proposals. Then, the voters will not be able to judge the economic impact of the programmes. They can do no more than make back-of-the-envelope calculations. Maybe they can not even judge whether the figures presented to them by the political parties are correct or misleading, if they are presented at all. Given that the economic impact of the programmes is unclear, their political aspect is likely to dominate voting decisions. For instance, voters are ready to judge on the impact of euthanasia, or gay marriage, without having facts and figures. Voting on the decision to enter the EMU becomes somewhat more difficult, and voting on tax rates is rather irrational if party-neutral figures are not available. So, the lack of figures is more or less a problem, depending on the issue at hand. This line of reasoning suggests that in the Netherlands the economic aspect of political parties' programmes plays a relatively large role, compared to the many countries which lack a public calculation procedure. Is the Netherlands a country of traders and bureaucrats?

After the elections, the parties elected in parliament have to arrange a cabinet with a governmental agreement. In order to make a good match, the programmes are again compared, and this time the economic impact is not only useful but indeed crucial. After all, the cabinet has to prepare a budget plan for about four years and the room for manoeuvre is mainly an economic issue. Since in this hypothetical situation there are no calculations by CPB in advance of the elections, such calculations will be done afterwards, during the cabinet formation process. That is to say, only the coalition parties will have the economic impact of their programmes assessed during the formation process. Still, the impact calculation is likely to lengthen the negotiation phase.

Given that in the second stage some of the parties have to reveal the economic impact of their programmes, the information becomes available sooner or later anyhow. However, the parties which are confident on the favourable outcome of their programme have an incentive to reveal this in advance of the elections. Parties whose own calculations turn out less favourable, hereafter called parties with "bad economic programmes", have an incentive not to reveal the economic impact of their programmes. They may have good reasons to nevertheless stick to their programmes. For instance, they may prioritise the economic impact below other effects, such as ethical or environmental effects. The programmes of smaller religious parties give examples of family politics, the principal rejection of moving towards the 24-hour economy, or taking care of the earth as given to mankind, which may result in lower economic outcomes than other parties' programmes. As long as those small parties serve a group of voters who share the prioritisation and thus vote for the party irrespective of the unfavourable economic figures, this may be a smart strategy. The same line of reasoning holds for smaller leftist parties which make a strong case for socialism or environmental protection. Still, those parties have to face that the economic impact figures of their programmes are not favourable to the public at large.

The notion that the parties which are confident on the favourable outcome of their programme have an incentive to reveal their figures before the elections, indicates the existence of a coordination problem. It can be sketched as in the tables below. In each cell, the outcome to the party with the sound economic programme is given first. The Nash equilibria are in bold type.

Table 1: Hide or reveal (generalised case)

		Party with bad economic programme	
		Reveal economic impact	Hide figures
Party with sound	Reveal economic impact	$a+b$, $a-b$	$a+b$, 0
Economic programme	Hide figures	0, $a-b$	0, 0

with a = pay-off reveal, $-a$ = pay-off hide, b = pay-off sound figures, $-b$ = pay-off bad figures.
If a party chooses to hide, the impact effect is absent so that b becomes zero in all cells.

Table 2: Hide or reveal (hide effect dominates impact of figures: $a=2>b=1$)

		Party with bad economic programme	
		Reveal economic impact	Hide figures
Party with sound	Reveal economic impact	**3, 1**	3, 0
Economic programme	Hide figures	0, 1	0, 0

Table 3: Hide or reveal (impact of figures dominates hide effect: a=1<b=2)

		Party with bad economic programme	
		Reveal economic impact	Hide figures
Party with sound economic programme	Reveal economic impact	3, -1	**3, 0**
	Hide figures	0, -1	0, 0

Table 1 gives a generalised version of the coordination problem. The cells in the tables are described bottom-up. The situation in which neither party reveals its figures is taken as neutral. This starting point reveals the situation in which voters are not used to receiving and processing figures, so they take their voting stance irrespective of quantitative information by voting on the basis of political rather than economical aspects of the parties' programmes. Moreover, if a party chooses to hide, there is no impact of the figures by definition, so that the pay-off becomes zero. If only the party with the sound programme hides its figures, it misses the opportunity to prove the soundness of its programme. Instead, it signals that something might be wrong, because it is the only party who does not show figures. The party with the bad economic programme has little incentive to reveal its figures, since they are not favourable and cannot be compared to those of other parties. If the party with the sound programme reveals its figures while the party with the bad programme does not, the first party gains both from the positive impression of the figures and from the positive effect of revealing figures as such. The party with the bad programme will be seen as having something to hide, so it is worse off as compared to the situation in which neither party reveals its figures. In the case with both parties revealing their figures, the signalling effect is irrelevant. Here, the opposite effect of the figures themselves is clearly visible.

Table 2 gives the situation in which the effect of revealing or hiding the figures has more impact than the figures themselves. The pay-offs are such that the upper left cell is a Nash equilibrium. Here, the signalling effect dominates the impact of the figures as such, so that the party with the bad economic programme is worse off when hiding its figures.

The situation in which the impact of the figures is dominant, represented by Table 3, has a Nash equilibrium in the upper right quadrant. If the party with the sound programme hides its figures, then the party with the bad programme will do likewise, but if the second party decides to hide its figures, the former party has an incentive to reveal its figures. If the party with the sound economic programme chooses to reveal its figures, then the party with the bad programme has an incentive to hide, while the other way around holds as well. Thus, the situation in which the party with the sound programme reveals its figures while the other party does not, is a Nash equilibrium. The situation in which both parties reveal their figures is not a Nash equilibrium. This outcome hinges upon the assumption that the negative impression of "having something to hide" is smaller than the negative impact of the figures as such.

From this raw sketch of the incentives, it can be concluded that the parties with the best economic programmes have an incentive to reveal the figures of the impact calculations before the elections. Irrespective of the capacity of the audience in processing the economic information, following the incentive is a sign of having a good programme, while hiding the figures is a signal of having a bad one. No conclusions can be drawn on the relative impact of the figures as such as compared to the impression that is created by hiding or revealing one's figures. This issue is empirical in nature, and has to do with the psychology of the voter. Does the voter judge a party on the simple fact that it does or does not participate in an impact calculation procedure or does the voter judge on the basis of the exact figures which result from such calculation?

3. IN PRACTICE

The actual situation in the Netherlands is such that the impact of the programme is calculated. This leaves little opportunity for testing the games above. However, a recent offer of CPB to expand the calculation may provide some kind of laboratory experiment.

A few months ago, CPB again realised that its calculations were rather quantitative in nature, with the micro- and macroeconomic model variables being rather limiting with respect to particular political issues such as the health care sector and the environment. CPB offered to involve other institutes in the process, which could better address these issues. The impact of programme issues on the environment could be calculated by the National Institute of Public Health and the Environment (RIVM), while programme issues on education and health care could be analysed with separate models built by CPB itself. The coordination issue discussed above on hiding or revealing can now be put to the test.

While the leftist PvdA and the slightly rightist CDA favoured the add-ons, the rightist VVD was strongly opposed to the idea (NRC Handelsblad, 2001). VVD spokesman Visser argued that the calculations would be too qualitative in nature, and therefore the political standpoints of the parties could not be assessed by such calculations. Remarkably, he made clear that the rejection did have nothing to do with possibly negative outcomes of the calculations for his own party. His VVD colleague Zalm declared that CPB is good in calculating the impact of policy measures, but that health care is within the political rather than the economic domain (Banning and Kalse, 2002). CDA spokesman Wijn took a rather principal stance by referring to the initial agreement to have the calculation done, either for all parties or for none. Seen from the perspective of the tables above, this point of view may reveal insecurity about the outcomes of the calculations for the own party, which differ according to which type of party the CDA turns out to be (NRC Handelsblad, 2001). The PvdA seems to consider itself a party with a sound programme on the environment, health care and education, since its spokesman Crone said: "We have nothing to hide". He later declared those parties who do not have their proposals on health care reform calculated by CPB cowards (Banning and Kalse, 2002). The more leftist parties GroenLinks and SP also favoured the add-on calculations. Says Kees Vendrik of GroenLinks: "If you don't join, you lose the debate on the feasibility of your programme in advance" (Lambregtse and Scheer, 2002). In the nineties, it was difficult for GroenLinks to accept that the main features of its programme were not taken into account in the model calculations according to their own ideas, but the recognition the party gained because it had submitted the programme to the CPB calculation procedure was worth the while. Here again, the signalling effect of having one's programme calculated, dominates the impact of the particular figures that result from assessing the programme. The Olympic adage seems to apply: participating is more important than winning.

It may therefore be concluded that the incentive to reveal impact calculations is strongest for those parties who have sound programmes, both in (game) theory and in practice. Also, the impact of the figures themselves may be less than the signalling effect as such. The above remarks by the several parties' spokesmen support this suggestion. Thus, in terms of the tables above, Table 2 best reflects reality. The reveal/hide effect dominates the impact of the exact figures, so that the Nash equilibrium is (reveal, reveal). The election campaign of 2001-02 supports this conclusion, since then even eight parties had their programmes calculated.

4. THE CALCULATING INSTITUTE

The phenomenon of revealing the high level of quality one stands for, is not unique to political parties. It is common to many situations of asymmetric information and can also be seen in shops or with service providers. Examples are the network of car repair shops ("Bovag"), the association of movers ("Erkend verhuisbedrijf"), a butchers' association ("Keurslagerij") and some of the franchise formats. Here, the reputation mechanism provides self-management of quality by disciplining those who wish to use the reputation mechanism.

These associations need an institution to monitor the members and the quality of their goods or services. This can be done by peer review, such as retailers visiting each other's shops and publicly reporting about the visit, or by a centralised institute which they collectively pay for. The latter has the advantage of being independent of the member who monitors or is monitored, so that the tendency to centralise the monitoring is understandable. In the case of political parties in the Netherlands, several institutes could do the job. One could think of parliament, which has its own small research institution. Other possibilities are the research institutes NYFER, with its experience in transforming political issues into economic calculations, OCFEB (Erasmus University of Rotterdam), with its close link to the policy making process, the knowledge centre for trade and industry SMO, which already assessed the non-economic issues in political programmes (Schouten, 1998), and of course CPB, which has a solid reputation of calculating by use of economic models.

However, parliament's own institute is too small, NYFER is unwilling to do the job since it does not believe in total impact calculations (Banning and Kalse, 2002), OCFEB serves different purposes than competing with CPB, and SMO is more societal than economically oriented. CPB differs from the other institutes because its calculations are taken into account in the policy making process. CPB's assessment of the current economic situation is a common starting point for all parties involved.[3] However, the choice for CPB has its disadvantages to the extent that non-economic issues are difficult to deal with in its models. This disadvantage does not relate to CPB in particular, but to impact calculation in general.

5. PROS AND CONS OF CALCULATIONS

The (late) eighties and early nineties can be interpreted as the age of economization.[4] Perhaps the growing interest in the economic outcomes of election programmes can be interpreted as belonging to the economization movement.[5] The economic impact calculations started in 1986 with the programmes of the three main parties CDA, PvdA and VVD. D66 followed in 1989 and GroenLinks submitted its programme in 1994. Given that CPB does the economic impact calculations of the election programmes, what are the advantages and disadvantages of the procedure? The answer to this question may indicate who profits most from the calculation, because those who profit most will experience the advantages while the disadvantages will be felt by those who do not profit from the calculations.

In the argument above, the calculation procedure was treated as a black box, with the election programmes being put in, and with economic figures coming out. Not surprisingly, it was then concluded that the parties with the best programmes in terms of economic soundness would profit most by the calculation procedure, which gives them nice figures they can reveal to the voters. This conclusion partly hinged upon the assumption that the calculation with the CPB model(s) gives a "good" impression of the economic impact of the particular election programme. As was seen above with GroenLinks, some parties doubt this assumption. In this section, the black box will be opened a little so that the characteristics of the calculation procedure can give a more precise clue about its benefits.[6]

Advantages

An undisputed advantage of centralised calculations by a qualified institute such as CPB is that they provide a foundation for a rational and well-documented discussion.[7] The methodology of the calculation is checked and is uniform across the parties. For all programmes, the same baseline scenario is taken as a starting point, so that the exogenous variables have the same values.[8] Because the programme issues have to be translated into parameter values for the CPB model(s), the parties have to be exact in formulating their intentions. For instance, they cannot get away with simply wishing to reduce subsidies without making clear which subsidies they wish to reduce and by what amount.[9] The calculation thereby also makes clear what has to be paid or foregone in order to achieve a particular result. Thus, the political and economic discourse is disciplined by the calculation procedure. Parties with sound figures have an easy job and favourable outcomes, while parties with less solid proposals have a hard time. All numbers are checked and only realistic figures are taken into account in the calculations.[10]

However, this advantage may have a drawback insofar as it implicates that CPB is the umpire who decides on the realism of the figures (Van Bergeijk, 1998). Deciding upon realism is not always a matter of objectivity, as disputes among empirical researchers show. Last year's dispute between CPB director Henk Don and the economists of GroenLinks, also indicates that realistic assumptions are not a matter of objectivity, but of intersubjectivity at best.[11] Nevertheless, the test on realism by

CPB does filter out what can seem attractive to the layman, but is considered unrealistic once scrutinised by economists. Thereby, the difference between "sound" and "bad" figures becomes clearly visible. The political parties receive feedback on their programmes, both in detail and in the overall effects. This may bring them to revising their programmes before the election, which can improve the quality of the programmes. Parties with economically doubtful programmes are likely to profit most from this second chance. The option of such a revision round is facilitated by the uniform presentation of the outcomes of all programmes.[12]

The voter may also benefit from the uniform presentation, which may take the form of a timetable indicating where one is likely to end up if a particular party gets elected. However, this effect depends upon the voter's ability to understand and interpret the figures. Finally, as was indicated earlier, the calculation procedure makes the coalition formation easier and more transparent. As Den Butter and Mosch put it:

> "Those policy measures [...] have the best chance to be included in the government agreement that have, according to the calculations of the CPB, the largest favourable effects on the major policy goals".[13]

Disadvantages and limitations

But what are these "major policy goals"? If political parties do not agree about their goals, such as the amount of reduction of the government deficit, comparing the parties' programmes becomes difficult (Van Bergeijk, 1998). Even if they would agree, the calculation has its drawbacks and limitations. According to Van Bergeijk and Haffner:

> "A major drawback is the fake precision of the calculations, which has several causes. One is the imprecision which is inherent to economic models. The outcome of the impact calculations may be such that two parties' programs have results that differ thousands of jobs, so that the job issue becomes a hot topic in the election campaigns rather than being mere incidents of limited precision of the models."[14]

Differences in model outcomes may lie within the confidence intervals, so that criticism should not focus on the model but on the decision not to refer to such intervals.[15] These issues may be difficult to explain to laymen, but the voters cannot be assumed to understand such intricacies themselves, so this requires a communication effort.

Another source of fake precision refers to the baseline scenario, in which the values of exogenous parameters like the international economic developments are very likely to change during the years to come. Since the rest of the world has a large impact on the small open economy of the Netherlands, the calculation should not be read as a forecast. Fortunately, it does not limit a comparison of the programmes, since this is based on a baseline scenario which is uniform across parties.[16] However, this aspect needs careful communication to the laymen voters, in particular in times in which the baseline scenario is no longer adequate, as was the case in Spring 2002.[17]

Another limitation of the calculation is that it is supposed to reveal the effects of election programmes for the cabinet period to come. However, for most policy measures the time needed to fully take effect is much longer. For some measures the costs precede the benefits, while for others the opposite applies. This information is highly relevant to those who wish to judge the programmes. Depending on the time horizon of the political parties and the voters, the presence or absence of such information is more or less advantageous. In the past, CPB solved this issue by providing outcomes on the medium term of four years as well as on the longer term of eight years, but the most recent impact calculations do not include such forward projections (CPB, 1994 and 2002).

Some limitations of the procedure also have their advantages. For instance, the fact that CPB only takes those measures into account which can be decided upon by the party once it participates in the cabinet, has the advantage that possibly unrealistic assumptions about actions of other entities are eliminated automatically. For instance, parties cannot anticipate upon decisions of the European Commission which would be favourable to their goals.[18] However, the drawback is that reactions of other economic agents on policy measures may be neglected as well. For instance, it is difficult to model the behavioural impact of changes in the marginal wedge, and the change in behaviour of private agents to the deregulation measures is invisible.[19]

This limitation of the impact calculation procedure may become a disadvantage to political parties who wish to propose large or institutional changes instead of incremental changes in the way the budget is created and spent. For those parties, the calculation procedure loses its neutrality since it provides a disincentive on large or institutional changes. To prevent this non-neutrality, CPB could pay more attention to elements which cannot be quantified, such as institutional reforms, as well as to the uncertainties which are inherent to the quantitative results.[20] This recommendation goes further than CPB's own suggestion that politics should not limit its discussions to CPB's figures.[21]

A last category of drawbacks refers to the process of convergence between the parties' programmes. All parties have to present their programmes in such a way that CPB can translate it into parameter values for the model(s) it uses. Therefore, parties have to conform their terminology and way of estimating impact to a standard. To this extent, the convergence is unavoidable. The fact that several kinds of measures cannot be included in the model(s), makes it unattractive for parties to diverge on really large issues. Moreover, it can also result in election programmes being customised to CPB model(s) rather than the model(s) being made suitable to analyse the programmes. Given the fact that no model is perfect, the policy making process might become biased by the imperfections of the model(s). This drawback can be solved partly by adding other calculations, as CPB and RIVM proposed to the parties. Another measure is the political and societal comparison of the election programmes as performed by the SMO (Schouten, 1998). This admittedly subjective comparison is complementary to the rather objective economic calculations by CPB. Finally, it should be noted that large mistakes in the baseline scenario would affect all parties equally, but depending on the particular aspect of the scenario involved, some parties may be worse off than others.

6. THE VOTER

Given that the political parties profit from the impact calculation because their programmes become better underpinned, what is the benefit to the voter? Academic economists should prevent projection here, by taking into account that only six percent of the voters are academic, and that the average intelligence quotient is one hundred by definition. The voter thus cannot be assumed to know terribly much about the workings of the economy, let alone compare figures provided by CPB.

Moreover, the voter faces uncertainty regarding the business cycle and the economy as a whole. Uncertainties about his or her own economic situation make it difficult to disentangle the impact of policy measures on a country as a whole from the influence on one's own situation. The fallacy of composition is difficult to resist at election time. To sum up, voters have limited comprehension and economic rationality. This makes it likely that economists overestimate the impact of the CPB figures to the typical voter.

This need not be a cause of concern. The difference between economics and politics, which was touched upon earlier, would plea for a voting process which is not determined by economic aspects alone. Not all aspects of life are economic in nature and those who are not at home in economics may be better in distinguishing other aspects of election programmes. The SMO publication mentioned earlier might be a better "societal timetable" to those people. Issues such as safety, peace and war, justice, and liberty, are not firstly economic in nature. Education and health care, the proposed add-ons in the impact calculation, are in between. They can be considered victims of economic imperialism or subjects of economization, depending one one's point of view.[22] It might also reflect the interest in economic issues as a cultural trait of the Dutch.

They do have their costs and benefits, however, and at least the costs can be calculated. The voter could be informed about those, so that he or she has at least some idea of the price ticket of particular measures. The annual costs of a cell in jail as compared to the costs of an extra policeman may help in judging parties' claims on the net effects of both measures. However, the benefit of returning home safely every evening cannot be expressed in budget figures. The voter is likely to perform subjective valuations of political variables, sometimes helped by opinion leaders who translate the figures in political terms.

7. CONCLUSION: WHO BENEFITS?

Recently, the former member of parliament Hans Jeekel wrote:

> "Those election programmes, and all the calculations, are a Dutch ritual no voter is waiting for. However useful they used to be, in fact it is a manifestation of the bureaucratic orientation of our national politics."[23]

Is Jeekel right? Taking stock of the arguments presented above, two functions of the impact calculation remain. Both functions have their own groups of beneficiaries.

The one function is to provide objective information to the voter, who can thus compare the election programmes of political parties. The procedure followed by CPB secures that only technically realistic policy proposals are taken into account and that all programmes are compared on the basis of the same scenario. These features make the outcome of the calculation procedure a trustworthy comparison of the economic impact of the programmes. However, it is doubtful whether the typical voter is capable of understanding and interpreting the information provided. Understanding the workings of the economy may be difficult, but understanding the way in which figures about it have to be interpreted, with all accompanying limitations to exactness, is surely too demanding. Therefore, to the voter, the reveal/hide effect dominates the impact of the figures themselves.

The other function is to improve the process of programme writing by the political parties and the process of cabinet formation afterwards. Here, those involved are capable of understanding and interpreting the information, and the outcome of the calculation procedure provides them with the figures which are necessary to agree on a cabinet agenda (governmental agreement). Negotiations which are based on the same assumptions regarding the state of affairs and the workings of the economy are more likely to result in commonly wished for outcomes. To those involved, the impact of the particular figures is more important than the reveal/hide effect.

Table 4: The benefits of impact calculation for two groups

	Political parties	*Voters/ Taxpayers*
Reveal / hide	Pay-off depends on quality of programmes	Signalling effect of soundness
Figures	Calculation facilitates improving the programmes	Useful to some, too complicated for many Efficient cabinet formation process, better policy making

The benefits from impact calculation are roughly summarised in Table 4. The costs are borne by the taxpayers and the benefits differ across the two groups involved. From this argument, the conclusion follows that CPB would do no harm by focusing its communication about the calculations to the parties involved, rather than to the general audience. However, given that not all politicians are economists, careful communication on what can and what can not be concluded from the impact calculation, may remain necessary. The voters may feel well-informed by only knowing which parties did have their programmes calculated and the main conclusions from the procedure. As taxpayers, they also profit from the better programme formation process and the faster agreement on a sound cabinet agenda. All in all, the calculation may be worth the while also to them, but this requires empirical cost-benefit analysis.

NOTES

1 Den Butter and Mosch (2001), p. 10.
2 De Kam estimates the costs at eight person-years, or 700,000 euro per election (De Kam, 2002).
3 Commissie Beleidsgeoriënteerde Toetsing van het Centraal Planbureau (2001), item 20, p. 11.
4 Grit (2000), p. 4.
5 If that were true, then a change away from economization may be marked by increasing dissatisfaction with the economic impact calculation. The broadening of impact calculation by inclusion of "qualitative" impact assessments on health care and environment might indicate such movement.
6 The costs are easier to assess, from the CPB budget plan and the political parties involved.
7 Haffner and Van Bergeijk (1994), p. 497.
8 Zalm (1994), p. 7.
9 Zalm (1994), p. 7.
10 Zalm (1994), p. 7.
11 See www.economie.nl (Discussie/Reacties/2001/Groeiramingen) (in Dutch).
12 Zalm (1994), p. 8.
13 Den Butter and Mosch (2001), p. 10.
14 Haffner and Van Bergeijk (1994), p. 497.
15 *Cf.* Haffner and Van Bergeijk (1994), p. 504, and Commissie Beleidsgeoriënteerde Toetsing van het Centraal Planbureau (2001), item 29, p. 14.
16 Zalm (1994), p. 8.
17 Van Cann 2002, and Don (2002), p. 8.
18 Zalm (1994), p. 8.
19 Van Bergeijk (1994), p. 504.
20 Commissie Beleidsgeoriënteerde Toetsing van het Centraal Planbureau (2001), item 37, p. 16-17.
21 Zalm (1994), p. 9.
22 *Cf.* Grit (2000).
23 Jeekel (2002), translation mine.

REFERENCES

Banning, C., and E. Kalse (2002), Oppermachtig in Den Haag ("Supreme in The Hague"), *NRC Handelsblad*, 25 March

Bergeijk, P.A.G. van (1998), De wonderbaarlijke terugkeer van de inverdieneffecten ("The Miraculous Return of Positive Knock-on Effects"), *Economisch Statistische Berichten*, 83(4148), 313-314

Butter, F.A.G. den, and R.H.J. Mosch (2001), *The Dutch Miracle: Institutions, Networks and Trust*, Alert Research Memorandum 2001-18, Amsterdam: Vrije Universiteit

Cann, G. van (2002), Politiek partijen vrijwillig in keurslijf van CPB ("Political Parties Voluntarily in the CPB Straitjacket"), *Het Financieele Dagblad*, 25 March

CPB, 1994, *Vijf verkiezingsprogramma's, Economische gevolgen van voorgenomen beleid.* ("Five Election Programmes. Economic Effects of Proposed Policy"), The Hague: Sdu Uitgeverij

CPB, 2002, *Keuzes in kaart 2003-2006. Economische effecten van acht verkiezingsprogramma's*, ("Charting Choices 2003-2006. Economic Effects of Eight Election Programmes"), The Hague: CPB

Don, F.J.H. (2002), Ten Geleide ("Preface"), in CPB (2002), *Keuzes in kaart 2003-2006. Economische effecten van acht verkiezingsprogramma's* ("Charting Choices 2003-2006. Economic Effects of Eight Election Programmes"), The Hague: CPB, 7-11

Grit, K. (2000), *Economisering als probleem* ("Economization as a Problem"), Assen: Van Gorcum

Haffner, R.C.G., and P.A.G. van Bergeijk (1994), The Economic Consequences of Dutch Politics, *De Economist*, 142(4), 497-505

Jeekel, H. (2002), Haags taalbehang zit de gevestigde politici in de weg ("Veiled Language of The Hague Stands in the Way of the Established Politicians"), *NRC Handelsblad*, 15 March

Kam, C.A. de (2002), Verslingerd aan het Planbureau ("Mad About CPB"), *NRC Handelsblad*, 23 April

Lambregtse, C., and P. Scheer (2002), Gevangen in cijfers ("Caught in Figures"), *Forum*, 4 April, 10-14

NRC Handelsblad, 2001, *Halt aan doorrekenen VVD-program* ("A Halt to the Assessment of the VVD Programme"), 21 November

Schouten, C.W. (1998), *SMO-verkiezingsboek. De vijf grootste politiek partijen langs de maatschappelijke meetlat* ("SMO Election Book. A Societal Measure of the Five Largest Political Parties"), SMO 98-2, The Hague: SMO

Zalm, G. (1994), Ten geleide ("Preface"), in CPB (1994), *Vijf verkiezingsprogramma's. Economische gevolgen van voorgenomen beleid* ("Five Election Programmes. Economic Effects of Proposed Policy"), The Hague: Sdu Uitgeverij, 7-9

CHAPTER 8

OTTO H. SWANK

A RATIONALE FOR ASSESSMENTS OF ELECTION PROGRAMMES

1. INTRODUCTION

The consequences of many policies are complicated and difficult to foresee. In the Netherlands, CPB Netherlands Bureau for Economic Policy Analysis (CPB) assists the government with assessing the consequences of economic policy. In addition, CPB calculates the economic consequences of party programmes before each election for parliament. The main objective of this chapter is to provide a rationale for the latter practice.

This chapter consists of two parts. The first part addresses the question whether or not direct democracy leads to informed policy decisions. Point of departure of the analysis is Condorcet's Jury Theorem (CJT), which, loosely speaking, says that when a group of individuals has to make a binary decision by simple majority rule, nobody should be excluded from voting (Section 2). CJT is often referred to as a justification for the principle of majority rule.[1] I argue that CJT hinges on the assumption that signals are for free. Once agents have to expend effort on receiving an informative signal, CJT completely collapses (Section 3). This part of the chapter gives a rationale for representative democracy. Decision making under direct democracy is likely to be based on little information (Cukierman and Spiegel, 1998). The reason is that information is an (impure) public good. The provision of this good raises a free rider problem. A possible way to solve this free rider problem is to delegate the making of policy to a limited number of agents.

In the second part of this chapter, we examine a model in which two political parties compete for office (Section 4). These parties cater for the interests of their constituencies. In addition, they receive rents from holding office. There exist two

Johan J. Graafland and Arie P. Ros (Eds.), Economic Assessment of Election Programmes: Does it Make Sense?, 97-106.

alternative models of the economy. We assume that the free rider problem as to information collection is solved in the sense that both parties know which of the two models is the correct model of the economy. However, in line with part one of the paper, voters are ignorant. They do not know the correct model of the economy. We argue that when voters do not have incentives to collect information, parties have an incentive to supply it. Unfortunately, parties are inclined to provide incorrect information. They will adopt a view of the economy that is meant to increase their chances of winning the elections. The outcomes of the model are inefficient for two reasons. First, uncertainty about policy outcomes may distort voting behaviour. The party that wins the election may differ from the party that would have won the election under known policy consequences. Second, parties may adapt policies to support the (sometimes wrong) information they supply to voters. Consequently, policy is based on incorrect information, even though politicians are assumed to know policy consequences.

All in all, this chapter shows that it is unlikely that democracy alone, direct or representative, leads to policy based on a proper amount of information. An institution like CPB may help to solve this problem. In addition, the practice of calculating the economic consequences of election programmes may prevent parties from manipulating information in order to increase their chances of winning the elections.

Sections 2 and 3 are based on the literature on CJT. As mentioned before, this literature gives a justification for majority rule. According to Piketty (1999), CJT should get the same status in political science as the Arrow-Debreu result in economics. In the same spirit, Ladha (1992) speaks about a theoretical explanation for the strength of democracy. A less optimistic paper on CJT is written by Austen-Smith and Banks (1996), who argue that allowing for strategic behaviour undermines CJT.

Section 4 is based on the literature on model uncertainty. Part of this literature revolves around the question how policy makers should deal with policy uncertainty. Brainard (1967) shows that uncertainty about policy effects of instruments on targets should lead to a conservative use of instruments. Christodoulakis and Van der Ploeg (1987) demonstrate how conflicting views can be pooled into a compromise model. Once this model has been derived, the policy problem can be formulated as a standard optimization problem. The other part of this literature deals with the question how policy makers actually deal with model uncertainty. There is some consensus that policy makers differ in their views on the economy and that these views are connected with their political preferences. In the United States, Republicans seem to have more faith in the invisible hand than Democrats and less faith in government intervention (Harris, 1962, Tobin, 1974, and Tufte, 1978). Letterie and Swank (1998), Roemer (1994), Swank (1994) and Schultz (1995) provide an explanation for these observations.

2. CONDORCET'S JURY THEOREM

We consider a community of n, $i \in \{1,2,\ldots,n\}$, members. These members have to make a decision about a public project, X. The project can be implemented (X=1) or rejected (X=0). There are two states of the world, $S \in \{-h, h\}$. Each state occurs with the same probability. The members have identical preferences over decisions and states. They are represented by:

$$\begin{aligned} U_i\left(X=1 \middle| S=h\right) &= h \\ U_i\left(X=1 \middle| S=-h\right) &= -h \\ U_i\left(X=0 \middle| S=h\right) = U_i\left(X=0 \middle| S=-h\right) &= 0 \end{aligned} \qquad (1)$$

Equation (1) implies that all members prefer implementation to status quo when the state of the world is h, but prefer status quo to implementation when the state of the world is $-h$.

The decision about the project is made by majority rule. Each member of the community votes either for implementation or for status quo. We assume that n is odd, so that implementation of the project requires that at least $(n + 1)/2$ members vote for implementation.

Members do not know the state of the world. However, before voting on the project takes place, each member observes a private signal, $s_i \in \{g, b\}$ about the state of the world. With probability $0 < \pi < 1$ a signal is fully informative:

$$\Pr\left(S=h \middle| s_i=g\right) = \Pr\left(S=-h \middle| s_i=b\right) = 1$$

With probability $1-\pi$ a signal does not contain information about the true state:

$$\Pr\left(S=h \middle| s_i=g\right) = \Pr\left(S=-h \middle| s_i=b\right) = \tfrac{1}{2}$$

In the present model, agents take one action: they vote. We assume informative voting, *i.e.* members vote in line with their signal. Therefore, members who receive signal $s_i = g$ vote for implementation, while members who receive signal $s_i = b$ vote for rejection.[2]

An important feature of the above model is that there is consensus among the members of the community that one of the two policy alternatives is the correct choice. The problem is that the correct choice is not known. Another important feature of the model is that individuals may make mistakes, but that each individual is more often right than wrong. When each member votes in line with his or her signal, the probability that member i votes for the correct alternative equals

$$\begin{aligned} p_i &= \pi + \tfrac{1}{2}(1-\pi) \\ &= \tfrac{1}{2}(1+\pi) \end{aligned}$$

Note that $\pi > 0$ implies that $p_i > \frac{1}{2}$.

Let us now calculate the probability that majority rule leads to the correct decision. This probability is equal to the probability that at least $\frac{1}{2}(n+1)$ members receive the correct signal:

$$P_n = \sum_{m=\frac{1}{2}(n+1)}^{n} p^m (1-p)^{n-m} \binom{n}{m} \qquad (2)$$

where P_n denotes the probability that in a community with n members at least $\frac{1}{2}(n+1)$ voters choose the correct alternative. From (2) we can derive the following Theorem:

Theorem *Let n (n odd) members choose by majority rule between two alternatives that have equal probability of being correct a priori. The members vote independently and all votes have the same probability of being correct, $p = p_i$, with $p_i > 0.5$. Then the more members there are, the more likely it is that a majority makes the correct choice.*

Proof: We have to show that $P_{n+2} > P_n$. Let

$$g(m,n) = \sum_{m}^{n} p^m (1-p)^{n-m} \binom{n}{m}$$

The following two rules are well-known:

$$g(m+1,n) - g(m,n) = -\, p^m (1-p)^{n-m} \binom{n}{m} \qquad (3)$$

and

$$g(m,n+1) - g(m,n) = p^m (1-p)^{n-m+1} \binom{n}{m-1} \qquad (4)$$

Using these rules, it is straightforward to show that

$$P_{n+2} - P_n = p^m (1-p)^{n-m+1} \binom{n}{m} \left[\frac{n+1}{n+1-m} p - 1 \right] \qquad (5)$$

Since $m = \frac{1}{2}(n+1)$ and $p > \frac{1}{2}$, $P_{n+2} - P_n > 0$. Q.E.D.

Theorem 1 is a variant of Condorcet's Jury Theorem (CJT). Loosely speaking, it says that it is inefficient to exclude individuals from participating in collective decision making processes.

3. ENDOGENIZING INFORMATION

An important assumption underlying CJT is that signals are for free. In this section, we show that relaxing this assumption has important consequences for CJT.

In the previous section, we made a distinction between informative and uninformative signals. The probability of an informative signal π was exogenous. In this section, we maintain the distinction between informative and uninformative signals, but assume that the probability that a signal is informative depends on the effort an individual has put in collecting information. We, so to speak, endogenize information. Formally, we replace π by $\pi(e_i)$, where e_i denotes the effort i has expended on collecting information. As to this function $\pi(e_i)$, we make the following assumptions: $\pi' > 0$, $\pi'' < 0$ and π(0) = 0. Effort is costly. The idea is that collecting information takes time. The costs of gathering information are reflected by $c(e_i)$, with $c' > 0$ and $c'' > 0$.

Apart from the inclusion of effort, the model of this section is similar to that of the previous section. The introduction of effort implies that each individual has to make two decisions. First, each individual has to decide how much effort to put in collecting information. Second, each individual has to make a vote decision. Once individuals have collected information, each individual faces the same problem as in the previous section. As before, we assume informative voting. When determining effort, each individual chooses effort up to the point where the marginal benefits equal the marginal costs. Clearly, *i*'s marginal benefits depend on the voting behavior of the other individuals. Only in case of a tie, *i*'s effort has consequences. The optimal effort level, e^*, thus solves

$$\left(p^{n/2}(1-p)^{n/2}\right)\binom{n}{n/2}\pi'(e)h = c'(e) \tag{6}$$

where $\left(p^{n/2}(1-p)^{n/2}\right)\binom{n}{n/2}$ denotes the probability that *i*'s vote is decisive. Application of the implicit function theorem to (6) shows that e^* is a decreasing function of n.[3] The implication is that the more individuals are added to the collective decision making process, the lower is the probability that an individual receives an informative signal. If $n \to \infty$, then $e \to 0$.

Endogenizing effort has thus important implications. CJT requires that $p > \frac{1}{2}$. Theorem 1 is based on the assumption that p is independent of n. We have shown that p is decreasing in n. Moreover, if n takes a very large value, then p goes to $\frac{1}{2}$. These implications are quintessential with large number of voters. With large numbers of voters, we should not forget the fundamental irrelevance of the individual voter. This notion is not novel. It goes back to Downs (1957), who used the insignificance of the individual voter to show why voters are (rationally) ignorant.[4]

Summarizing: endogenizing information has brought us back to rational ignorance. Rational ignorance is a strong argument against direct democracy. In fact, rational ignorance is the rationale for delegation.

4. PARTISAN VIEWS OF THE ECONOMY

Direct democracy is not common. Modern democratic societies delegate policy decisions to elected policy makers. Democracies are representative rather than direct. In the previous section, we have argued that policy making in direct democracy is based on little information. The question remains whether representative democracies perform better.

Politicians disagree. Some believe that the income tax should be more progressive; some think it should be less progressive. Some think that disability benefits should be reduced; some think they should be increased. Basically, there are two reasons why disagreements may arise. First, politicians disagree about the objectives, for example because they have different constituents. Second, politicians disagree about the consequences of policies. Disagreement about the consequences of policies is hardly surprising. As said in the introduction, the consequences of many policies are complicated and difficult to foresee. In the previous section, we have argued that citizens hardly have incentives to spend time and money on collecting information about the economy. However, in a world where different politicians offer different policies, voters can only make sensible voting decisions if they have some perceptions of the working of the economy. In this section, we argue that when voters do not have incentives to collect information, politicians have incentives to supply information. The reason is that in elections politicians want to sell their policies. Adopting a specific view of the economy may help selling policies.

Consider a group of voters whose utility depends on policy X and outcome Y. Assume the following linear-quadratic preference function:

$$U_i = Y - \lambda_i X^2 \tag{7}$$

where $\lambda_i > 0$ is the cost voter i attaches to X. Voters are heterogeneous. They differ in the cost they attach to X.

Two parties, L and R, compete for office. The party that wins the election determines policy. There are three alternatives $X \in \{X_L, X_{SQ}, X_R\}$, with $0 < X_L < X_{SQ} < X_R$. The reason for restricting the policy space to three alternatives is that voters may find it difficult to distinguish between subtle policy changes (Harrington, 1993). A straightforward interpretation of the policy space is that X_L means a cut in public spending, X_{SQ} refers to the status quo and X_R means an increase in public spending.

There are two models of the economy: $Y = r_1 X$ and $Y = r_2 X$, with $r_2 > r_1$. The true model of the economy $r \in \{r_1, r_2\}$ is revealed to the political parties, but not to voters. We assume that if $r = r_1$, then party L's most preferred policy is X_L, while R's most preferred policy is X_{SQ}. If $r = r_2$, then L's most preferred policy is X_{SQ} while R's most preferred policy is X_R.

The election outcome depends on the median voter's (M's) vote. If M votes for party L, all voters with $\lambda_i > \lambda_m$ vote for party L. Suppose that voters know the programmes parties will implement, if elected. Then, M votes for party L rather than for party R if

$$r_m X_L - \lambda_m X_L^2 > r_m X_R - \lambda_m X_R^2$$

implying

$$\lambda_m > \frac{r_m}{X_L + X_R} \tag{8}$$

where $r_m = \frac{1}{2}(r_1 + r_2)$ denotes voters' perceptions of the working of the economy. Now suppose that the position of the median voter is uncertain. Specifically, assume that λ_m is uniformly distributed over the interval $[-z, z]$. Then the probability that party L wins the election equals

$$\Pr(L) = \frac{1}{2z}\left(z - \frac{r_m}{X_L + X_R}\right) \tag{9}$$

Equation (9) reflects the usual properties of spatial voting models. The probability that L wins the election is an increasing function of X_L and X_R. The intuition is clear. An increase in X_L implies that the programme of L moves to that of R. In contrast, an increase in X_R implies that the programme of R moves from the ideal position of the median voter. For our purposes, the effect of r_m on the probability that party L wins the elections is most important. Clearly, this effect is negative, implying that party L wants voters to believe that X has a marginal effect on Y. Since the probability that party R wins the elections is simply equal to 1 – Pr(L), party R wants voters to believe that X has a huge effect on Y. To put it differently, party L will claim that model 1 is the correct view of the economy, whereas party R will claim that model 2 will be the correct model of the economy. Partisan or ideological views of the working of the economy will arise. Note that voters cannot infer the correct model of the economy from parties' statements about the working of the economy. As a consequence, the election outcome does not contain information about the working of the economy. If the median voter's preferences over parties change with the correct model of the economy, then this lack of information is a real distortion.

So far, the analysis has been based on the assumption that voters know parties' programmes. Let us now allow for the possibility that the party in office before the election can signal its information about the correct model of the economy. Formally, the extended model consists of two periods: a period before the election and one after. We assume that at the beginning of the game, nature chooses one of the models. The chosen model will describe the working of the economy, both before the election and after. Nature reveals its choice to both parties, but not to voters.

At the beginning of the game party L is in office. The analysis for party R is analogous. Before the election, party L chooses policy. After the election, the party that has won the election chooses policy. The main question is: Does the party being in office before the election base policy on the correct model?

Suppose $r = r_1$. Model 1 is thus the correct model of the economy. As a consequence, L's most preferred policy is X_L. Moreover, with reasonable assumptions about the way voters update their beliefs about the working of the economy, the choice of X_L does not make voters believe that $r = r_2$ is the most likely model of the economy. Thus, also from electoral considerations, X_L is L's most preferred policy.

Now suppose $r = r_2$. Now party L's most preferred policy is X_{SQ}. However, from X_{SQ} rational voters infer that model 2 is the correct model of the economy. If this information makes it more likely that the median voter votes for party R than for party L, X_{SQ} reduces L's chances of winning the elections. This reduces L's period 2 utility: rents from holding office will go to party R and party R will choose X_R. Thus before the election, party L may face a trade-off between a sub-optimal policy in period 1 and a sub-optimal (from L's perspective) policy in period 2. When party L cares sufficiently about holding office, it will choose X_L before the election.

Summarizing: in our model, asymmetric information about the working of the economy may have two adverse consequences. First, it may distort the election process. The "wrong" party may be elected, implying that policy does not accord with the policies preferred by a majority of voters. Second, parties may have an incentive to base policy on an ideological model of the economy rather than on the correct model of the economy.

5. CONCLUDING REMARKS

The main objective of this chapter is to provide a rationale for CPB's assessment of election programmes. We started the analysis with a study of representative democracy. We argued that direct democracy is unlikely to lead to policies that are based on a proper amount of information. In principle, the notion of rational ignorance provides a rationale for representative democracy. By delegation of policy to a limited number of individuals, the free rider problem concerning information collection can be solved. However, in Section 4 we argued that political parties have an incentive to manipulate information. The reason is that they have to sell their programmes to uninformed voters.

In Section 4, we made the assumption that parties know the correct model of the economy. The basic idea behind this assumption is that in a representative democracy the free rider problem concerning information collection can be solved. However, also in a representative democracy, time and money should be spent on information collection. We argued that parties may have incentives not to use the information about the working of the economy. The implication of this is obvious: when information will not be used, the benefits of information collection are zero. As a consequence, also in a representative democracy, policy makers do not have strong incentives to collect information.

It is easy to show that under a veil of ignorance, all agents want policy to be based on a proper amount of information. Of course, this result is not surprising. Since democracy, direct or representative, does not always give incentives to agents to collect information, charging an institution, like CPB, with collecting information about consequences of policy proposals is likely to enhance welfare. Clearly, in practice, it is not always easy to guarantee the independence of such a public agency. Wilson (1989) has argued that the reputation of a public agency is often established at its birth. A good or a bad start can be decisive.

NOTES

1 See *e.g.* Young (1988).

2 Austen-Smith and Banks (1996), and Swank and Visser (2002) allow for strategic voting.

3 Important is that $\left(p^{n/2}(1-p)^{n/2}\right)\binom{n}{n/2}$ decreases with n. Proof:

$$\left(p^{\frac{1}{2}(n+2)}(1-p)^{\frac{1}{2}(n+2)}\right)\binom{n+2}{n/2+1} = \left(p^{n/2}(1-p)^{n/2}\right)\binom{n}{n/2}p(1-p)\frac{(n+1)(n+2)}{(n/2+1)^2} \le \left(\frac{n+1}{n+2}\right)\left(p^{n/2}(1-p)^{n/2}\right)\binom{n}{n/2}$$

4 For a discussion, see Fiorina (1997).

REFERENCES

Austen-Smith, D., and J.S. Banks (1996), Information Aggregation, Rationality, and the Condorcet Jury Theorem, *American Political Science Review*, 90(1), 34-45

Brainard, W.C. (1967), Uncertainty and the Effectiveness of Policy, *The American Economic Review*, 57(2), 411-425

Christodoulakis. N, and F. van der Ploeg (1987), Macro-Dynamic Policy Formulation with Conflicting Views of the Economy: A Synthesis of Optimal Control and Feedback Design, *International Journal of Systems Science*, 18(2), 449-476

Cukierman, A., and Y. Spiegel (1998), *When Do Representative and Direct Democracies Lead to Similar Policy Choices?*, Center Discussion Paper No. 98115, Tilburg: Tilburg University

Downs, A. (1957), *An Economic Theory of Democracy*, New York: Harper & Row

Fiorina, M.P. (1997), Voting Behavior, in D.C. Mueller (Ed.), *Perspectives on Public Choice: A Handbook*, Cambridge (U.K.) *et cetera*: Cambridge University Press, 391-414

Harrington, J.E. (1993), Economic Policy, Economic Performance, and Elections, *The American Economic Review*, 83(1), 27-42

Harris, S.E. (1962), *The Economics of the Political Parties*, New York: MacMillan

Ladha, K.K. (1992), The Condorcet Jury Theorem, Free Speech, and Correlated Votes, *American Journal of Political Science*, 36(3), 617-634

Letterie, W., and O.H. Swank (1998), Economic Policy, Model Uncertainty and Elections, *Economics and Politics*, 10(1), 85-103

Piketty, T. (1999), The Information-Aggregation Approach to Political Institutions, *European Economic Review*, 43(4-6), 791-800

Roemer, J.E. (1994), The Strategic Role of Party Ideology When Voters are Uncertain About How the Economy Works, *American Political Science Review*, 88(2), 327-335

Schultz, C. (1995), The Politics of Persuasion When Voters Are Rational, *Scandinavian Journal of Economics*, 97(3), 357-368

Swank, O.H. (1994), Partisan Views on the Economy, *Public Choice*, 81(1-2), 137-150

Swank, O.H., and B. Visser (2002), *Delegation or Voting*, Tinbergen Institute Discussion Paper TI 2002-005/1, Amsterdam *et cetera*: Tinbergen Institute

Tobin, J. (1974), *The New Economics One Decade Older*, Princeton: Princeton University Press

Tufte, E.R. (1978), *Political Control of the Economy*, Princeton: Princeton University Press

Wilson, J.Q. (1989), *Bureaucracy*, New York: Basic Books
Young, H.P. (1988), Condorcet's Theory of Voting, *American Political Science Review*, 82(4), 1231-1244

CHAPTER 9

EDUARD J. BOMHOFF AND LEO VAN DER GEEST

FOOD FOR POLITICIANS, NOT FOR VOTERS

1. INTRODUCTION

Economists the world over are engaged in evaluating economic policy, but the Netherlands is the only country where election programmes are audited by an official office. So are the Dutch breaking new ground or is this just national folklore with dubious traits?

CPB Netherlands Bureau for Policy Analysis (CPB) dissected the electoral programmes of the country's political parties for the fifth time in succession recently (CPB, 2002). This chapter is a critique of such "auditing" of election programmes. First we examine what voters get out of it. That is: practically nothing. We then discuss the rationale of the exercise. That's chiefly anchored in the disciplining effect it has on the authors of those programmes. We then move onto a substantive criticism of CPB's methods, which leads us to conclude that those methods may seriously distort the Office's findings. Finally, we discuss the effect of the exercise on the behaviour of political parties.

2. FOR CONSISTENCY'S SAKE

In March 1998, the OECD published a review of (necessary) reforms of the Dutch economy (OECD, 1998), and in 1999 the International Monetary Fund published a comparable analysis (IMF, 1999). Two ministries – Economic Affairs, and Social Affairs & Employment – had already run an international comparison over the strengths and weaknesses of the economy of the Netherlands (Ministerie van Economische Zaken, 1998, and Ministry of Social Affairs & Employment, 1997). The *Global Competitiveness Report* (Porter *et al.*, 2000), and the *World Competitiveness Yearbook*[1] are two additional annual publications that contain a surfeit of information for comparing Dutch performances and shortcomings with the

Johan J. Graafland and Arie P. Ros (Eds.), Economic Assessment of Election Programmes: Does it Make Sense?, 107-112.

experiences of neighbouring nations. That sort of comparative analysis is an aid in approximating where Dutch performances lag behind and where there is room for improvement. In addition, it is often possible to provide a rough indication of the accompanying costs and benefits.

In our opinion, such an approach is also valuable when analyzing electoral programmes. The starting point is voter's needs, which are placed in an international context or historic perspective wherever possible. The next step is to examine how political parties respond with promises to voters. Experts, economists, columnists and most notably eleven million voters can then judge for themselves the nature of the wishes and the reality of the promises.

Every list of points on which the Netherlands falls short and could do better, given the performances of others or its own past achievements, is obviously subjective. Also promises made to voters can be evaluated in various ways. So CPB takes a different route, less sensitive to the invariable charge of subjectivity. It adds up the cost to the treasury of the various promises in the election programmes and attempts to estimate the corresponding consequences for inflation, wage movements and competitive position. Conceivably, the model may even go some way to revealing how the labour market will respond to these changes. But that isn't the information voters need to know. The CPB's audit of the electoral programmes fails to create insight into the strengths and weaknesses of the Netherlands in specific areas or to measure the nation's economy against pluses or negatives in other countries.

Does that mean that CPB's efforts are futile? In his introduction to *Keuzes in kaart* ("Charting Choices") CPB Director Don explains how CPB's analysis contributes to creating better insight into the content of electoral programmes and how they match up to each other. Parties are invited to elaborate and elucidate their programmes, which results in greater clarity on the ins and outs of their policy proposals. A party that achieves big savings on disability expenses is expected to clearly state whether the savings they make are down to changes in the size of benefits, eligibility criteria or the premium differentiation quotient. It is very probable that the self-discipline involved in allowing the party programme to be audited by CPB has a positive effect here: parties are forced to work out coherent proposals on government expenditures and revenues, because a shortfall exposed by the audit can open up the programme to attack. In that way, CPB's audit encourages the political parties to strive for consistency in their proposals.

3. IRRELEVANT TO REAL CHOICES

Electoral debates and media discussions show that the quality of health care, education, safety, infrastructure and the urban environment are important issues for voters. They want to know how the proposals tendered by the political parties contribute to improving those issues. On that point *Keuzes in kaart* has little to say. As Don argues in his introduction:

> "Too little is known about the economic impact of more education, more safety or more infrastructure, for example, aside from whether the policy proposals are sufficiently armored to survive in the real world."[2]

Further, he states:

> "The most important limitation on CPB's analysis is that the expected economic impact relates only to a few aspects of the broad political programme set out in the party programmes."[3]

These remarks are honest and correct, but offer no excuse to leave major consequences of some policy proposals out of consideration.

In working out the financial consequences of the policy proposals, CPB limits itself to the effects on the budget and on aggregate demand. In other words, the impact the proposals have on government income and how that affects national expenditure and the labour market. The programme effects (the impact the proposals have on improving the economy's performance) are not factored in, because too little is known of them. Yet these effects are the crux of almost every single policy proposal.

International polls show that managers grade the road and rail network in the Netherlands low, in comparison to neighbouring countries.[4] Though the Dutch motorway system has grown by only 13% in the past ten years, while mobility has swelled by over 25%, some political parties remain hesitant about constructing more roads.[5] The quality of service offered by Netherlands Railways has been noted. These issues may be very damaging to the Dutch economy, and extra investment could help limit that damage. International comparative analysis could shed light here. But there is no place in the CPB models for these programme effects, so the political parties score points for every euro they save on infrastructure related spending or subsidies for public transport. The costs are factored into the financial calculations; the benefits remain invisible for the model.

4. NO PROGRAMME EFFECTS

If the effects of programme promises of more education, greater safety or more infrastructure are not factored in because their dimensions are unknown, the whole analysis is affected: why should the figure zero always be considered the most probable outcome of these effects? In that event the conclusions of budgetary analysis are no longer correct either, due to widespread links between economic performance (growth, employment) and government finances. A model that attempts to interpret the impact on expenditure, while the figure zero is utilized for this kind of supply side effects, is like a wedding without a bride – of no use in serious analysis. A few examples will clarify this.

- *Safety*. With a police force of 45,000 the Netherlands is firmly nestled in the middle bracket in Europe. However, on average only 1,200 (less than 3%) of those 45,000 employees are available for evening and night work. If a political party were to propose rationalizing the situation by buying off the police force's refusal to adjust their working hours with a one-time pay rise – thus allowing many more police to work evenings and nights – then the costs incurred would have a negative impact on CPB's calculations, whereas there would be no seep of the positive consequences in terms of safety through to the Office's math. International studies show that house prices are sensitive to crime levels (Cullen and Levitt, 1996). Furthermore, households and companies alike have to take copious measures to protect themselves from car thieves, housebreakers, burglars, and retail & corporate crime. The costs saved by the private sector here have no place in the model.

- *Infrastructure and regional policy.* CPB's models do not contain a regional component. The lack of a less centralized perspective is fatal for any analysis of the costs and benefits of large infrastructure. CPB only factors in estimated travelling time savings in the benefits column. The standard works on cost-benefit analysis show that a calculation must be based on the projected consumer's surplus, as some households will attach much bigger value to a new travel option. Suppose that a new fast transport link is considered between the country's centre and a more peripheral region. It would then be incorrect to calculate the benefit of that fast link as the number of people that actually use this new transport mode multiplied by some tariff for the saved travelling time; the "option value" of the new transport link makes the consumer's surplus much greater.[6] Moreover, the costs of doing nothing have to be taken into account. If the new tranport link is not realized, this may result in higher congestion costs in the overcrowded centre region, for households (less room for houses, higher prices) as well as for firms. So, to calculate the consequences of such infrastructure projects, we have to estimate the consumer's surplus including option values and indirect effects for example on the cost of congestion. This is overlooked in the present auditing of electoral programmes, where the only benefit acknowledged in the gross operating result is the spending impulse that accompanies extra construction.

Another point of concern is that CPB does not highlight the costs involved with some drastic policy proposals. For example, in 1998 GroenLinks proposed that all civil servants be obligated to work 32 hours or less per week. In its text, CPB noted that this was a proposal with an entourage of risks, but these did not play any part in the audit. In the same electoral programme GroenLinks argued for fiscal penalties for all firms whose employees work longer than those 32 hours per week. Many economists would say that a measure of that caliber would dint the flexibility of companies confronted with rapid fluctuations in demand. The short working week also cuts down the return on education and development. That aspect was not addressed in the CPB models.

Another example is GroenLinks' proposal in 2002 to restrict energy consumption in the Netherlands in order to achieve the Kyoto objectives for 2010. International figures show that the Netherlands is an above-average energy-intensive economy; it consumes scarcely less energy per unit of gross operating result than the United States.[7] So the desire to make the Dutch production structure less energy-intensive can be well-founded. To achieve that goal, GroenLinks proposes a major shift in the tax system (18 billion euros!), in favor of labour-hungry sectors and to the detriment of energy-intensive industries. That would have significant consequences for, say, the bonded warehouse function of the Dutch economy and our truck farming industry, both of which contribute to the relatively high energy-intensity of the Dutch economy. CPB provides no figures from abroad giving any indication whether that sort of adjustment will be easy or tough to introduce, or whether jobs will be lost in shrinking sectors faster than they are created by companies that are not required to pay as much tax. Yet CPB is quite sure that the impact on employment will be only 0.08 % (5,000 jobs). No doubt an international sample can offer some raw data that may help us quantify the policy options on this issue, but we fail to see how a model exclusively for the Netherlands can ever work out the risks our nation runs when, on the back of major shifts in the tax system, relative prices change in the Netherlands, but not in neighboring countries.

5. ADVERSE POLITICAL EFFECTS

Politicians know that any unfavourable CPB evaluation will be hammered in during the election and may lose them votes. They invest efforts in arming their programmes to withstand this test. Besides tricks to bamboozle the model, there is a tendency for the various parties to ensure their programmes blend in with the crowd to avoid being "picked off" by CPB. The electoral debate becomes a skirmish about decimals, with consequences for democracy that need to be addressed.

Additionally, it's hard to find any differences in the model's results for economic growth as presented by the eight parties and the bureaucrats, who are responsible for the baseline scenario. The gap between the champions of growth of the VVD and the growth-reducers of GroenLinks is no more than 0.3% a year (0.7% structurally). In terms of job creation (in people terms) there is no significant difference between these two parties. The question is how a party like GroenLinks could be within touching distance of the VVD in terms of economic growth and job creation in 1998, and continues to be so in 2002. Do these parties not have varying degrees of enthusiasm for growth and profit?

6. CONCLUSION

CPB's calculations can help force political parties to keep their proposals consistent, but they are irrelevant with respect to real political choice. The analysis of budgetary and expenditure effects also only reveal part of the picture, which is therefore inaccurate, because the programme effects of policy proposals (the actual target of the measures) are usually set at zero. Ultimately, the submission of programmes of political parties to the judgment of civil servants, albeit voluntarily, under pain of damaging their reputations as a serious party, results in a restriction of options and political discussion, which does not serve democracy.

Our alternative is to identify weak areas in the national economy through international comparisons and to assess which measures could help us improve these weak areas by studying the experiences of other countries.[8] Such assessments can be accomplished by various independent organizations, preferably outside the government. A major advantage of such an approach is that all suspicion of political interference in the assessment can be ruled out. In addition, more competition in the policy evaluation process may improve the quality of evaluation and contribute to a more lively political debate.

NOTES

1 Annually published in *Management Services*.
2 CPB (2002), p. 9, our translation.
3 CPB (2002), p. 10, our translation.
4 Porter *et al.* (2000).
5 In the period 1990-99 the combined mileage of the Dutch motorway system rose by 13%, compared to 36% in France, and as much as 108% and 262% respectively in the two fastest growers Finland and Ireland. The Netherlands is ninth out of fifteen EU member states in this period.
6 See for example Boardman *et al.* (2001), for a discussion of consumer's surplus and for example p. 480 for an analysis of "conurbation effects".
7 See Porter *et al.* (2000), p. 65, for the figures and the relationship to prosperity per head of the population. Esty and Porter's article in this book places the Netherlands in eighteenth place among forty countries in terms of the amount of energy consumed per unit of gross operating result. The US is in twenty-second place; twelve European countries score better than the Netherlands, including Switzerland, Denmark, France, Germany, Spain, Finland, Sweden and the United Kingdom.
8 NYFER is preparing such an approach; publication is expected shortly after the election of 2002.

REFERENCES

Boardman, A.E., D.H. Greenberg, A.R. Vining, and D.L. Weimer, (2001), *Cost-Benefit Analysis. Concepts and Practice*, 2nd ed., Upper Saddle River: Prentice Hall

CPB (2002), *Keuzes in kaart 2003-2006. Economische effecten van acht verkiezingsprogramma's* ("Charting Choices 2003-2006. Economic Effects of Eight Election Programmes"), The Hague: CPB

Cullen, J.B., and S.D. Levitt (1996), *Crime, Urban Flight and the Consequences for Cities*, NBER Working Paper No. 5737, Cambridge MA: NBER

IMF (1999), *The Netherlands Transforming a Market Economy*, Washington DC: IMF

Ministerie van Economische Zaken (1998), *Toets op het concurrentievermogen* ("Benchmarking the Netherlands"), The Hague: Ministerie van Economische Zaken

Ministry of Social Affairs & Employment (1997), *Social Policy and Economic Performance*, summary document for a conference organized by the Netherlands' presidency of the European Union, The Hague: Ministry of Social Affairs & Employment

OECD (1998), Implementing Structural Reform: A Review of Progress, in OECD, *Economic Surveys, Netherlands*, Paris: OECD, 59-76

Porter, M.E., J.D. Sachs, A.M. Warner, C. Moore, J.M. Tudor, D. Vasquez, K. Schwab, P.K. Cornelius, M. Levison, and B. Ryder (2000), *The Global Competitiveness Report 2000*, New York *et cetera*: Oxford University Press

CHAPTER 10

HERMAN H.H. VAN ERP

THE DEMOCRATIC QUALITY OF ELECTIONS

1. INTRODUCTION

CPB investigates, broadly speaking, the economic effects of the realization of various political parties' programme intentions. The goals of the programmes, or of economic policy in general, are not under discussion. The significance that is usually attributed to CPB research illustrates the very dominant position of the economy in present-day politics. The part the impact calculus plays in the elections is largely determined by the prestige economic analyses have gained in politics. Economics has grown to control public life more and more. From home economics it evolved into state economics, but nowadays the economy is almost a synonym of the basic system on which society functions, and economics ranks as the pre-eminent social science. This orientation of politics on economics implies a narrowing down of the importance of the political as such, as I have amply demonstrated elsewhere.[1] I shall approach this orientation critically in a number of propositions, but at the same time accept it as a fact which all thinking on political functioning must take into account.

If philosophers were asked to subject political party programmes to analysis and evaluation, their questions would be different from those CPB asks. Political-philosophical investigation of a programme should focus primarily on the question whether the intended goals and effects are respectable in the light of political justice. The questions this chapter addresses to political philosophy, however, do not concern the way in which it would analyse political programmes, but the way in which it evaluates CPB's type of research. The starting point of this evaluation too ought to be a more general idea of the political, and it should be conducted in the light of political morality and justice. The information the CPB impact calculus yields, is in nature a means to promote the quality of the political process. My contribution starts from the question whether CPB research is an adequate means to promote the quality of politics. As a specific philosophical question it does not deal

Johan J. Graafland and Arie P. Ros (Eds.), Economic Assessment of Election Programmes: Does it Make Sense?, 113-125.

with the effectiveness of the means and the cost involved, but with the value of the means in the perspective of the way in which we pursue political justice. In reality it boils down to the question whether CPB research is significant for a good democracy. Democracy needs to justify itself in the perspective of the notion of the common good. *Grosso modo* it is my opinion that under specific conditions CPB research can contribute to this legitimation.

2. DISCIPLINE RATHER THAN INFORMATION

Economically justified action is not a formal economic concept, but a moral-political one. It is a demand for political justice, since it will not do to do justice at the expense of others. The means to spend are restricted; the money must be found somewhere and cannot be spent more than once. It is only a matter of common sense, therefore, to presume that the kind of impact calculi and comparisons CPB wants to make are decidedly called for and appropriate. Legitimate action requires that one pictures the costs involved in the realization of political desires. The electoral programmes of political parties can be criticized if they do not formulate clear policy goals and only present a mere list of desires without any calculation of costs. Such programmes would be built on quicksand.

Parties whose programme has been subjected to the CPB impact calculus may gain prestige from it. It gives them an image of a sense of responsibility, solidity and frankness. As a matter of fact, it is very hard for the voters to judge whether that image is legitimate. The CPB research is unintelligible for the average voter. The media may be able to draw some general conclusions from it, but to most people the informative value of the numerical comparisons remains pretty insignificant. They are not able to check whether the prestige a party gains from it is legitimate. The impact calculus has informative value for a small group of experts only, so that voters just have to trust that the way in which conclusions are drawn from the data in the political battle is indeed relevant and honestly carried out to boot. Anyway, a not too naive voter knows that various interpretations are possible and that all of them can be criticized one way or another. The figures must indeed turn out evidently negative for a party before the voter's trust in this party will be shaken. It is not to be expected that any party would run such a risk. In formulating their programmes parties will make sure that the outcome of an impact calculus will not be negative. This way the CPB impact calculus certainly has a preventive and steering effect. The CPB impact calculus lends party programmes an image of economic solidity. *This image is founded on supplying discipline rather than information.*

3. PRICE TAGS VERSUS COMMITMENT

The content of political party programmes can hardly be the direct object of an investigation that is interested in realistic prognoses. The very issue of the predictive value is not that relevant in the broader perspective of making explicit the political character of programmes. Electoral programmes give little hold to predict what parties will accomplish in the political process. Apart from the caprices of historical developments and the unpredictable outcome of a legislation on a European level, in the Netherlands the necessity to form coalitions can be blamed. Parties are well aware of this, and can always plead these aspects of the political process as an excuse for not completely realizing their plans, without provoking severe sanctions from the voters. It is understandable that the large extent of noncommitment of this political game of promises elicits irritation. It is equally understandable that the political dissatisfaction on this subject can be rallied and exploited. Programmes which make any impact calculus impossible because they only contain action items, can present this as a form of political panache since they pretend to quash bureaucratic thinking.

From a pragmatic point of view, questioning its predictive value reduces the importance of the impact calculus of programmes. *The predicting value of the impact calculus is small and of little relevance.* Can one demand from parties that they put a price tag on their political desires in advance? Is whatever they are willing to pay not the natural outcome of the political process of negotiation and decision-making? It is unconceivable that in a situation of war a government should be prepared or compelled to reveal in advance information about the expenses it is prepared to make to achieve war goals. In doing so it would not only be playing into its opponent's hand, but also moderate the political principles that justify the war by putting a price tag on them from the very start. A government can announce in advance that it will not use immoral means. But it cannot define in advance how much money it is prepared to spend or which other economic efforts are acceptable. A war economy will have to budget just as any other, even though this will probably happen in all secrecy. It is obvious that every set goal must be looked at in the light of a cost-benefit analysis of the means required to achieve it. But if in war high priority goals are abandoned because of the costs, this must definitely point to an emergency situation, unless there is something wrong with the will to really reach that specific goal.

In a comparable way one can argue that in a more normal political situation, it also holds that parties do not have to be prepared to pin exact figures on the means they are willing to summon for their high priority goals. In the first place, this does not fit in with the idea of high priority. Principled parties will therefore have more difficulties to include the goals which are of great political or moral importance to them in a cost-benefit calculation model. Parties of a more pragmatic stock will leave room for negotiation on most of their objectives. But even then it is often unattractive to commit oneself to definite figures, not only because, as we saw before, no predicting value can be attached to it, but also because the public setting of goals in various target figures can have a detrimental influence on the negotiation strategy in the process of forming coalitions. Only in a political system in which it is to be expected that only one party will be able to fully implement its programme, could such a programme be fitted with a more or less realistic budget.

4. NEUTRALITY OR IMPARTIALITY?

The CPB research seems to approach politics from the point of view of a socio-economic policy which has to be interpretable in financial terms. If this works, the policy obtains the label of solidity. CPB aims at giving information on the economic means political parties will employ, by means of a neutral investigation. As such it functions as a significant but merely formal economic instrument parties can use to their advantage when drawing up their programmes, and probably even more when looking for compromises in view of a governmental agreement. It is a means that fits more and more in the policy sphere, and therefore it seems to me to be an illusion to think that such information should carry much relevance in the making of specific *political* choices which ought to precede policy implementation. The question of how political parties deal with economic matters cannot be reduced to the disciplining question whether they make sensible use of their means in accordance with certain well-defined economic expectations and standards. The differences between parties do not only effectuate from economic choices in the sense of balancing taxes and expenditures, but also from different approaches of the economy as such. This kind of difference ought to be expressed much stronger in the impact calculus of the programmes. I am under the impression that these differences only emerge incidentally, like footnotes explaining why such peaks can be observed in some parties' entries.

The CPB calculators struggle with the notion of neutrality. They aim at providing a politically neutral instrument, and they think they can find it in these neutral, that is to say purely economic, numerical data. This however immediately raises the question of how politically neutral an appeal to economic neutrality can be. Economic solidity is not a politically neutral notion. *The CPB research would add to its political relevance if it would let itself be guided by an ideal of impartiality rather than by the methodical principle of neutrality.* If one recognizes that politics can look at the instrumental character of economy and economic analyses in many different ways, the question arises whether economic means can be perfectly neutral and whether the pursuit of neutrality is all that desirable. The desirability of neutrality introduces in politics itself much too easily a kind of liberal prejudice, since it almost always concerns a neutrality regarding individual preferences. Just like in economics these preferences must be respected as a kind of pre-given material, in the light of which specific collective goals must be considered as secondary. It is better to pursue impartiality instead of this neutrality. Impartiality means that one has to meet the desire of political parties to make their specific objectives also apparent in the numerical data and in the comparisons based on them. Impartiality implies a notion of fairness in which the relative importance of interests and goals must be taken into account, and can therefore not be put on a par with neutrality.

If within the framework of the CPB impact calculation there is a mention of economic effects, it usually concerns the effects on the economy in a restricted, specific sense. Economy then refers to a notion of social welfare inasmuch as it can be expressed in a model of expenditures and revenues. The more value is attributed to such calculations, the more important it becomes for political parties to have the goals they pursue for the sake of this welfare discounted in this model one way or another, to prevent it from functioning as a Procrustean Bed. Detrimental effects of environmental pollution can be visualized to some extent in the quantity of CO_2 emissions. To GroenLinks it was important to include numerical data on this subject in the model. Even though this does not provide an insight in the way in which this can be discounted in the calculation of the costs, the economic relevance of the effect has at least been acknowledged. To other parties other data would be desirable. But stressing impartiality in this way rather than predictability and numerical comparability, probably renders the CPB research too complicated.

This example clearly shows that what is to be understood by economic effects of programmes is subject to political discussion and cannot in advance be defined or restricted to effects that can be expressed in financial figures. However, by including more variables the model becomes increasingly more complex and expensive. At the same time it becomes less manageable for making comparisons that can put the economic solidity of parties to the test, since economic solidity does not yield a criterion which is neutral and independent of political choices. This shows that an optimal use of the calculus model is susceptible to inherent tensions that are not of a mere technical nature and cannot be solved purely on the basis of a cost-benefit calculation either.

5. POLITICAL PARTIES AND FLOATING VOTERS

One of the central questions in this chapter is whether the CPB impact calculus of election programmes promotes the quality of the elections. This is a rather complex question, since the goal and the quality of the elections can be judged in quite different ways. Within economic thinking the majority principle is mostly used in a utilitarian sense: good is what increases the satisfaction of needs of as many people as possible. The majority principle then functions as a policy principle: the well-being of the majority outweighs that of a minority. This principle has little to do with genuine democracy, because even a dictator or a small elite can govern within the perspective of the advancement of the majority of the population. This variant of democracy *for* the people can of course be combined with democracy *by* the people. Nevertheless the question remains whether the majority has a clear view on which policy is the most advantageous. Therefore, economic information on policy options is necessary, but as argued above, it is doubtful whether this can be very effective. Anyway, I do not think that CPB offers its service from this understanding of democracy.

Against the utilitarian use of the majority principle as a policy principle, one could pose the democratic use of the majority rule as part of a procedure to reach a political consensus.[2] In a procedural democracy the application of the majority rule does not mean that the interests of the majority are of greater importance, but that a majority has the right to decide which measures will be taken in the light of the common good. Applying the majority rule does not mean either that the majority is right, but that every individual vote carries equal weight. The legitimation of the rule is based on the idea of fairness, because it departs from the presupposition that in this way freedom and equality get their fullest due in case of a difference of opinions. Democracy then means that minorities are offered every chance to put forward their interests and their vision on the common good, and to canvass individual votes for it. This notion of a fair democracy implies that not every majority that enforces its will can be called a democratic majority. A majority that has eyes only for its own interests applies the majority rule in a problematic way.

The significance of the programmes for the electoral process is not unambiguous. Social choice theories honour the view that the voters' individual preferences regarding various political issues must be expressed in the election result. To be able to vote for alternative programmes that have the character of policy intentions is then a major aspect of the democratic choice process. Political parties are considered as coalitions or interest groups and their programmes as packages of policies and wants.[3] The rationale of political programmes and representative democracy is reduction of bargaining costs.[4] Some theories seem to regard it as a restraint on democracy that votes must be cast on parties and their programmes, because it seriously restricts the freedom of voicing preferences for each measure separately.[5] If the idea were correct that it would be more fair in a democratic view to vote on every individual issue, political parties would make sense only as some kind of pre-selectors of choices, without which the whole procedure of choosing would become impracticable. It is not unthinkable that the CPB research supports this view on democratic elections. Anyway, it promotes a reading of programmes that does not do justice to their function as "reasonable political conceptions" or particular implementations of the common good, preparing for just legislation.[6] In the comparison of programmes on a list of items the political identity of a party is not the object of special attention. It is for the individual voter to decide whether this is an important issue.

It is the more remarkable therefore, that all incumbent parties in the Netherlands agreed to submit to this CPB operation so unanimously, since the specific identity of parties is almost entirely lost in the research report. Parties disappear behind a multitude of figures, which reveal but small relative differences most of the time. The report can contribute little or nothing to the consolidation and continuation of the bond between a specific party and its voters. In the comparability of parties the value of the existence of such a bond is rather put into perspective. The voter takes it for granted more and more that he feels addressed as a floating voter. He is seen as a consumer who can pick and choose between a number of large brands or supermarkets which have been scrutinized by the consumers' organization, but who is of course aware of the fact that there still exist small shops which may have their own advantages and charm. Faced with this huge mass of floating voters the parties may profit from pertaining to the large brands and to exhibit themselves as such.

In the above views on elections it is taken for granted that we choose representatives of the people on the basis of programmes that meet our own desires regarding the realization of more or less concrete political goals. There are of course opposing views. According to Schumpeter, it is an illusion that politics can operate by presenting complex political programmes to the population to judge and choose. Democracy is a kind of open market in which everyone can compete for political positions of power. In this view, elections are a combat for canvassing votes for certain candidates who should inspire confidence as to their political competence.[7] This approach takes another view on the quality of the electoral process. In keeping with Schumpeter, programmes have a merely strategic function to canvass followers for a party or a candidate, and they play a clearly subordinate role with respect to content. If Schumpeter is right, parties will use the CPB research only in their struggle for power. *Because it is not at all clear from what exactly the impact calculated programmes gain prestige, the CPB research threatens to become a plaything in the electoral battle*. In CPB's view, this is decidedly not the part it ought to play.

6. THE QUALITY OF THE ELECTORAL PROCESS

The quality of the elections can be related to the result, to the procedure and to the circumstances under which they take place. Some critical remarks can be made regarding the concern over election results. Politicians often claim that the voter is always right. If this would be true, the quality of the election result could not be under discussion. As a matter of fact, however, this is an empty slogan. Good counselling and information can indeed improve the quality of the result of individual choices. In principle the CPB research can have a favourable influence on the quality of election results by giving objective information. But, as I have argued before, the information value of the research – insofar as it has the nature of a whole of predictions – has little relevance for the voter in determining his choice. There are negative effects too. As already mentioned, there is a tendency to reduce the political debate to a legitimation of policy measures in which increasingly more importance is attached to economic arguments. The economic effects linked to it measure the sense of legislation. The concern for the results entails that an assessment of the proper value of the political process through which those results may be affected, is neglected. Democracy, however, has in the first place to do with the quality of the process, not with the quality of results. That is the element of truth contained in the adage "the voter is always right".

The quality of the electoral procedure has to do with fairness in particular. With procedure I do not only refer to its rules and regulations and how they are applied by the government, but also the way in which parties and voters can make use of them. Voters for instance can vote strategically: they do not give their vote to a small party they prefer, but to another, larger party in order to reduce the relative electoral profit of a third party. On this kind of behaviour CPB has no influence. The significance of the CPB research for the fair character of elections is very indirect, since the investigation concerns the quality of the programmes, not the quality of the electoral procedure itself. But parties too play the strategic game. The extent to which they can take up a strategic position is limited by their willingness to draw up programmes that are susceptible to impact calculation. The quality of the elections certainly does improve if the alternatives offered to the voter are more reliable.

Another quality aspect relates to the circumstances in which elections take place, which might be positively influenced by the CPB research. The willingness of parties to submit those parts of their programmes that are of direct importance to economic policy to an impartial investigation, creates an atmosphere of mutual trust, openness and readiness for discussion. Those are the preconditions to make democratic elections more than a mere kind of struggle for power. The most important effect of the CBP research is that it draws the attention of politics to its responsibility for this economic reality. Thanks to this kind of research, democracy, at this culminating point of election time, becomes a form of communication too in the light of a desirable employment of means. But this also involves a certain degree of danger. Within the concept of a pluralistic democracy, the notion of politics is formalized, and with it the distinction between goals and means. The political aspect is more and more translated into a system of procedures, which has to guarantee a fair exercise of power within the boundaries of an already more or less well-ordered society. The notion of fairness, too, is highly encapsulated by economic theories. Politics then mainly emerges as an instrument of power to implement measures which, through surveying individual needs and preferences, can be supported and legitimated by figures. This way a very tight, intrinsic bond develops between economics and politics.

Politics threatens to be reduced to a kind of alternative and counterpart of the market force. Popular discussions on home affairs are for the greater part concentrated on the dilemma of more or less governmental influence on the economy, and in political comments in the media electoral programmes are still often seen as instruments to win votes for a certain economic policy. This is not only a matter of vulgarisation. Experts too describe the effects of political measures increasingly in economic terms of profits and losses and make them the subjects of game theoretical analyses and prognoses. In economic analyses, politics loses much of its own content and importance and becomes a formal concept itself, merely referring to struggle for power, strategy and the overcoming of prisoner's dilemmas. The political debate takes place chiefly in an atmosphere of pragmatic considerations, which places it outside the context of political values and standards. As the impact calculus takes place just before the elections, it helps preserve the image that politics is first of all about the economy. *In respect of the dangers of becoming a plaything in the electoral debate and of narrowing the political perspective to economics, it is probably more functional not to connect the CPB investigation too strongly to elections.* Making the loss and profit figures transparently needs to be placed in a broader frame, if it wants to benefit the quality of democratic elections.

7. THE CPB ANALYSIS AND THE POLDER MODEL

A healthy economy attunes ends and means to one another in a pragmatic way. Ever since the development of the welfare state, economic advice has strongly influenced the political choice of specific goals. More formally, this kind of economic knowledge can be defined as knowledge on the efficient use of means without getting into financial trouble. The more the economy itself has turned into a financial affair, the more rigid standards it appears to be setting to political action. With this the need to formulate a political vision on the nature and the validity of economic standards becomes more and more compelling.

In spite of the multiple views one can have on the relationship between politics and economy, it is possible to a certain degree to make a distinction between solid economic planning and irresponsible squandering and blundering. However doubtful the predictive value of the CPB analyses may be, one thing nevertheless remains: the objective information concerning the content of programmes in the form of numerical models can be a useful instrument to counter some programmes being used merely strategically or demagogically. Even if we disregard the informative value of the numerical comparisons of the programmes, the disciplining action of the operation remains. Parties, however, which are not prepared to submit themselves to this discipline, for whatever reason this may be, can in fact derive arguments to their advantage from this refusal. The importance that is attached to the CPB impact calculus can be criticized for being the expression of the accountant's mentality which dominates politics more and more. A rebellious party can proclaim that this kind of discipline suffocates the political *élan*. The CPB research can figure as a typical institution of the Dutch polder model. The expression "polder model", however, loses its positive denotation more and more, and calls forth associations with lackadaisical politics, back room consultation and the united party of the Netherlands Ltd. A discussion on the value that has to be attached to the disciplining effect of the operation quickly and irrevocably lands in hot ideological water, since it is typical of politics to define the relevance of economic effects and how to deal with them. It remains to be seen whether we can picture an efficient economic planning without presupposing any kind of political or moral choice. Economic and political perspectives converge and support each other. But political responsibility is much more than a kind of sensible management. The analysis of political party programmes should put into words in particular how a political party wants to give shape to this further reaching form of responsibility.

Economics is not a mere neutral means at the service of politics, as politics imply a well-defined vision on the importance of economic affairs. The CPB analysis could be important for information about parties' economic visions. To this end, however, the research must present itself rather as an analysis of the programme's consistency and soundness than as an economic prediction regarding anticipated effects. Showing the costs of the implementation of party programmes is of little significance to the voter, since the full implementation of a programme is highly improbable. We may assume that a party programme is more than a list of desired measures. In a programme a party tries to stress its distinctive political features by legitimating concrete political choices on the basis of general starting points, and to get the voters' support for them. These starting points may be very explicit or not quite so; they may have the character of fundamental principles or of more pragmatic rules. The impact calculus can reveal how a party would like to translate its starting points in concrete measures, and what it is prepared to pay for it. In certain cases it can bring starting points to the light that do not feature explicitly in the programme itself. This way it can serve as a clarification of the economic vision of the party, and as a touching stone of its political consistency and of the degree in which this consistency is expressed in economic solidity. *The less the CPB calculus focuses on comparing hypothetical results of the impact calculus, and the more it centres on the principles which found the differences that appear from these comparisons, the more meaningful it becomes.*

8. MEANS AND ENDS

Between economic goals and the common interest there are no striking incompatibilities as to their content. Politics determine their relationship. Following the classical scheme of ends and means, it is the economy's task to provide means and to contribute to an optimal fulfilment of human needs, whereas the characteristic feature of politics is that they must formulate the goals of a societal life of free citizens, which means guiding and standardizing the needs. The relationship between economics and politics is perceived as a means-ends relationship. Politics need to set goals and to stimulate the production of means in the interest of the common good and to distribute fairly the joys and burdens.

According to Plato and Aristotle, politics that only serve the satisfaction of needs cannot but threaten the common good. From this point of view they both had an aversion for democracy, since they saw it as a form of government that was more or less the mirror image of tyranny. Just like the individual tyrant confuses the affairs of the state with his own interests, in a democracy each individual tries to satisfy his very own needs.[8] Tyranny is the dictatorship of one over all; democracy leads to anarchy, unless demagogues manage to give shape to another form of dictatorship, *viz.* the dictatorship of the masses. The enlightened founders of our liberal-democratic ideals, Spinoza, Locke, and Kant, were also hesitant about such mass dictatorship. For them, good governement is not a sake of satisfying personal wants, but characterised by the rule of law.[9] They can be characterized rather as republicans than as democrats in the modern sense of the word. The republican tradition emphasises the autonomy and priority of politics in relation to the economic and social domain.

Social democracy translates its political ideals for the greater part in economic measures, which aim at combatting social inequalities without upsetting economic balances too seriously. Consequently, the distinction between political and economic goals becomes rather confused. When democracy is translated as an egalitarian satisfaction of needs of as many people as possible, the line between politics and economics becomes paper-thin. The classical means-ends relationship can easily be reversed within a formal approach of politics, reducing politics to a policy at the service of the economy. Many social theoreticians applaud this process for being a sign of the emancipation and liberation of the civil society from politics dominated by ideology. In my opinion it becomes problematic if politicians should stress from this very perspective the importance of neutrality and the normative character of the economic view.

Hegel characterizes the economic system of civil society as making reciprocal use of each other in order to satisfy one's own individual needs. In this *System der Bedürfnisse* everyone presents himself of his own free will as a means for others and uses others for his own purposes.[10] If society were to be reduced to this perspective of individual satisfaction of needs, nothing much can come of the realization of the ethical principle that every person counts as a goal in itself and can therefore never be used only as a means. Nevertheless, only from this perspective is it meaningful to formulate specific ends in politics, and legitimate to realize these ends, as elements of the common interest, with common means. It should be a task of politics to formulate values and goals in such a way that they do not succumb to this relativizing reflexivity of ends and means, but are placed in a perspective of priorities that are defined by a vision on the common good. Economic and political perspectives converge and support each other. But political responsibility is much more than a kind of sensible management. *The analysis of political party programmes should put into words in particular how a political party wants to give shape to this further reaching form of responsibility.*

The CPB research hardly highlights the vision of parties on the economic aspect of politics. The very way in which the investigation is presented prevents it. To elucidate the relevance of those visions, we must look differently at the means-ends relation between economics and politics. This other view can be illustrated with a metaphor. The relation of politics and the economy is comparable to the relation between an artist and his material and instruments. Material and instruments are means which do not only have a purely external relation to the work of art. The artist can play with the means-character of his material and instruments in the way he lets them be present in his work of art. Paint and sound are the materials with which a painter and a composer realize their work of art, whereas the brush is a much more external means than the material. Musical instruments seem less external, but a brushstroke too can be distinctly present, whereas a composition can exist without there being a live performance. The use of the means has a technical as well as an expressive aspect. In the same way the economy is the material as well as the instrument through which and in which politics realizes itself for the greater part. It is an obstinate and polyvalent means. How to handle it skilfully, is an art which cannot be defined by purely economic patterns, let alone by a mere technical-economical view on social life, exactly like the quality of a painting will not be determined by the quality of the paint.

9. SUMMARIZING CONCLUSION

Looking back, I see three lines of reasoning in this chapter. The first states that the CPB research carries great significance for parties but hardly any for the voters. This significance is situated in the disciplining effect rather than in numerical information. A side effect is that the given information starts playing a role of its own in strategic discussions. It would be sensible to consider unlinking the research somewhat from the electoral battle.

The second line of thought concerns the significance of democratic elections. Does the CPB operation not confirm an approach of elections in which they are stripped of their specific political meaning in no negligible way? There runs but a thin line between politics and economics, and both ought to be directed towards the common interest. It is precisely this fading boundary which demands that political visions be formulated on the relation between politics and the economy. In my opinion this is the point of political programmes. It seems that this aspect of the programmes can only be reflected poorly in the approach of this kind of research.

The third line of thought is a critique on the neutrality of the ends-means relation, starting from which the research seems to understand its own function. Even when admitting that the impact calculus does not have the character of a coffee grinder, since various models are used, the image of a Procrustean Bed remains. Parties keep feeling submitted to an economic operation which does no justice to their own vision on the economy. There is tension between neutrality, as a recipe with a liberal-economic stamp, and impartiality.

Can the CPB impact calculus have the character of an objective, impartial means serving politics as a whole, and not the specific interests of parties? I would like to finish with a cautious confirmation of this possibility. The hallmark of economic solidity functions as a counterbalance against political drivel, the pursuit of specific interests, reckless adventures and one-sidedness.

The fear for democracy turning into anarchy and demagogy has become less acute. Ever since the nineteenth century modern democracies have taken the shape of sufficiently stable states. But there is always the threat of demagogy. One of the side effects of the disciplining function of the CPB calculations is that it averts the danger of demagogy. The exhaustive information and financial justification of the various programmes fit within the concept of a formal, pluralistic democracy, which is even at right angles with the idea of democracy as a mass movement in which emotions and allegedly subjective interests motivate political choices. Research like the CPB's creates a climate in which various conceptions and implementations of the common good can be reflected on in a businesslike way, without one ideology defining in advance how this idea of the common interest should be dealt with. This creates room for political debate, instead of this debate being dominated by one overpowering economic ideology. To this end, however, it seems necessary to direct the CBP analysis in such a way that the political identity of the party programmes is pronounced more clearly. They should not as much be analysed as a compilation of policy measures, but be examined on their own economic consistency.

NOTES

1 Van Erp (2000).
2 For this distinction between majority principle and majority rule, see Van Erp (1999).
3 Riker (1962), p. 103 *ff.*; Van Deemen (1997), p. 124.
4 Barry (1990), p. 262 *ff.*
5 The necessity to vote for a political programme is a restriction of Arrow's first condition of fair choice: universal admissibility of individual orderings (*cf.* Arrow, 1963).
6 *Cf.* Rawls (1973), p. 360-362; Rawls (1993), p. 154 *ff.*
7 Schumpeter (1976), p. 278 *ff.*
8 Plato (1980), Book VIII, 562a *ff*, p. 302-305; Aristotle (1977), 1266a3, 1289b4, 1296a3, p. 107, 283 and 331.
9 De Spinoza (1994), chapter VIII and XI, p. 149 *ff.* and 220 *ff.*; Locke (1823), chapter XVIII, p. 457; Kant (1968), p. 352.
10 Hegel (1970), §§ 189 *ff.*, p. 346 *ff.*

REFERENCES

Aristotle (1977), *The Politics*, The Loeb Classical Library, Aristotle in Twenty-Three Volumes, Vol. XXI, London: Harvard University Press

Arrow, K.J. (1963), *Social Choice and Individual* Values, 2nd ed., New York *et cetera*: Wiley

Barry, B.M. (1990), *Political Argument*, (reissue), Berkeley *et cetera*: University of California Press

Deemen, A.M.A. van (1997), *Coalition Formation and Social Choice*, Boston *et cetera*: Kluwer Academic Publishers

Erp, H.H.H. van (1999), Democratic Pluralism and Majority Rule, *South African Journal of Philosophy*, 18(4), 347-355

Erp, H.H.H. van (2000), *Political Reason and Interest: A Philisophical Legitimation of the Political Order in a Pluralistic Society*, Aldershot *et cetera*: Ashgate

Hegel, G.W.F. (1970), *Grundlinien der Philisophie des Rechts*, Hegel Werke in 20 Bände, Band 7, Frankfurt am Main: Suhrkamp

Kant, I. (1968), *Zum ewigen Frieden*, Werke, Akademie-Ausgabe, Band VIII, Berlin: Walter de Gruyter

Locke, J. (1823), *The Second Treatise on Civil Government*, Works in Ten Volumes, Vol. 5, new ed., London

Plato (1980), *The Republic*, Book VIII, The Loeb Classical Library, Plato in Twelve Volumes, Vol. VI, London: Harvard University Press

Rawls, J.B. (1973), *A Theory of Justice*, new ed. Oxford *et cetera*: Oxford University Press

Rawls, J.B. (1993), *Political Liberalism*, New York: Columbia University Press
Riker, W.H. (1962), *The Theory of Political Coalitions*, New Haven *et cetera*: Yale University Press
Schumpeter, J.A. (1976), *Capitalism, Socialism and Democracy*, 5th ed., London *et cetera*: Allen and Unwin
Spinoza, B. de (1994), *Tractatus Politicus*, Sämtliche Werke Lateinisch-Deutsch, Band 5.2, Hamburg: Felix Meiner Verlag

CHAPTER 11

A. (TOON) VANDEVELDE

AGONISTIC DEMOCRACY AND THE CIVILISING VIRTUES OF PUBLIC DEBATE

1. INTRODUCTION

Politicians are more often lawyers than economists. The latter prefer to keep behind the scenes. They advise policy-makers rather than act for themselves. Probably this is not just modesty. Secretly the adviser of the prince cherishes the ambition to exercise more power or influence than those who decorate the public scene themselves, and this is even true for free-marketeers rejecting almost all government intervention in economic life. This background position entails various advantages and drawbacks. The adviser is not permanently in the picture. He does not have to face the critical questions and comments of the press as frequently as the politician does, but neither does he enjoy the applause of the larger public. If it comes at all, it will be destined for the politician. The man or the woman behind the policy-maker will at most get a discrete tap on the shoulder for his well-documented file. That should do. I heartily agree that the economists of CPB Netherlands Bureau for Economic Policy Analysis (CPB) have merited their tap on the shoulder. They have done an excellent job. But will they be heard? Is it useful for the general public to be able to learn approximately the cost of political options and electoral programmes? I will argue that after all it does make sense, but before coming to that conclusion, I will show that this is less evident than it seems at first sight. As the reader probably expects from a philosopher, I will raise other than just pragmatic arguments. My first point, therefore, relies on a somewhat deeper reflection about the very nature of politics.

Johan J. Graafland and Arie P. Ros (Eds.), Economic Assessment of Election Programmes: Does it Make Sense?, 127-133.

2. POLITICS AS ANOTHER SHOW?

There are – roughly speaking – two kinds of political philosophy. Some philosophers take political debate seriously. They declare the exchange of arguments on the basis of correct information to be the quintessence of politics itself. Others – less numerous, but not less challenging – deny that there is anything real at stake within the sphere of politics. Hannah Arendt, Michael Walzer, Charles Taylor and the American communitarians are associated with the first school of thought. Also republicans like Philip Pettit, partisans of participatory democracy, belong to it. The second school is mainly inspired by French post-structuralism. Jean Baudrillard, René Girard, Alain Lipovetsky, Michel Maffesoli and the theoreticians of "La société du spectacle" ("The Society of Appearances") belong to it. They tend to conceive society as a kind of phantasmagoria, dominated by the desire to distinguish oneself from the others, the desire to gain power and to defeat all rivals. Politics then is a show, in which substantial disagreements about ideas are utterly unimportant, as they are only an alibi for gaining the attention of mass media. In this conception politics obeys to the same logic as war. And the logic of warfare is well-known. Even if initially one of the parties in conflict is right, soon he will use the same methods as his adversaries. From the very moment on that a conflict breaks out, all parties become equal to each other. Violence is mimetic. It renders uniform those who resort to it. It's the same old story over and over again: anticommunism inspired by communist agitprop, anti-terrorist services using terrorist methods.

According to Baudrillard and his friends, political conflicts or political competition work out in exactly the same way. Of course, if one thinks so, there is no point in taking political programmes or electoral promises seriously even one single second. If the only message of all political parties is simply: "We are new and we are going to tackle things differently", then it is pointless to calculate extensively the cost of political promises. Moreover, it is hard to argue with people thinking in this vein. Popper would call their thought metaphysical, and coming from here, this is by no means a compliment. No experience, no events in the real world, can ever unbalance the theorist of the society of appearances. Each morning, when he looks up his newspaper, he finds new evidence of the futility of public debate. Hence this theoretical stance is irrefutable, but this has as a consequence that it is also relatively uninteresting. It starts from a bird's perspective. If one takes enough distance, then all human worries, conflicts and disagreements are indeed futile. From a cosmic point of view, nothing that happens on earth has any importance: the earthquake that makes thousands of victims is no more important than a scratch on my finger or an explosion on the surface of the sun.

Arendt, Pettit, Taylor and Walzer on the other hand, the second group of philosophers I mentioned, take the shared convictions of groups of people seriously. They think that the stories and arguments exchanged on the public forum are meaningful, that they are more than just a symptom of unconscious drives such as the urge to differentiate oneself. People want a good life, a just society, individual freedom, cultural and intellectual enrichment, but they disagree about the precise hierarchy of these values and about how they have to be realised. This indeed is the very substance of political debate. I tend to think that this second approach to political life is more interesting than the first one, but at the same time I have to recognise that there is some scientific research supporting the first approach, which is then no longer considered as a metaphysical a priori position, but rather as an empirical claim. This will be my second point.

3. ARE LEFT AND RIGHT DIFFERENT?

Paul de Grauwe, an economist from Leuven, has argued convincingly for Belgium that it is impossible to tell who was actually in power when one only looks at the historical record of various economic parameters. For a long time in Belgium, we had an alternation of left of the centre and right of the centre governments. Normally one would expect the former ones to raise taxes and to increase expenditures for social security. The latter on the contrary are supposed to diminish taxes and social expenditures. Actually – at least in Belgium – one sees exactly the reverse happening. I do not know whether this exercise has been done for other countries. It would be interesting to try it out for the Netherlands, a country with more or less the same kind of political alternation. The Belgian anomaly highlighted by De Grauwe can probably be explained. Leftist governments have to prove that they are able to respect the rules of financial orthodoxy and rightist ones have to pay a price in order to calm down the militant energies of trade unions and various other pressure groups.

Of course, De Grauwe's empirical data relativize heavily political debates about economic matters. However, this does not necessarily support Baudrillard's claim of the futility of all political debates. Maybe the Belgian example cannot be generalised. Maybe other, non-economic themes are (becoming) more important in the political debate. Some economists seem to think that a calculus of the cost of electoral programmes as it happens in the Netherlands, will stimulate political choices to be more or even mainly determined by economic policy. Free-marketeers will often reject that claim. Their argument runs as follows. In a globalising world, with a common European currency, a common European competition policy, a world in which some important economic policy levers and control mechanisms are increasingly supranational, national governments are mainly expected not to commit too many follies, not to create huge budget deficits for example, or not to break down spontaneous economic dynamism. A political party or a government that is unable to properly manage the economic system or that does not respect some minimal norms of decent management, will immediately be discredited and discarded from power.

This ultraliberal story turns into technocratic thinking if one tightens these minimal norms of decent policy so much that there are no political alternatives left. I think this is exaggerated. For thirty years now I hear ultraliberal economists explain that the price of a generous welfare state as we have it in Western Europe is prohibitive and that this is untenable in a small open economy like Belgium or the Netherlands, and nevertheless our extensive system of social security continues to exist and to offer opportunities and protection to many weaker members of our society. So there does seem to be some scope for choices in the domain of economic policy. Some will object that the recent entrance of green parties in European governments has actually changed very little to the logic of our highly polluting and wasteful economic system, but one may not put the stakes too high. Politics always change things slowly. Utopians are often too impatient and are therefore not well suited for political life. Hence politics is interesting for reformists, who believe modestly in the existence of small possibilities of jointly influencing the shape of social life.

I illustrate this with one last example. I cannot really prove this, but I am convinced that the success of extreme rightist parties in Flanders is partly – not exclusively – determined by the huge public deficits created in the seventies and eighties of last century. The necessity of reducing public debt in the nineties has increased taxes, has rendered public services very costly and has curtailed political creativity. Hence policy failures have a real cost. The quality of economic policy does make a difference and the CPB exercise continues to be relevant.

4. AGONISTIC DEMOCRACY

One can doubt whether electoral results have much influence on the exact composition of governmental coalitions – especially in a regime of highly proportional representation as in Belgium or the Netherlands. One can still have more doubts about the influence of elections and governmental coalitions on the exact shape of the policy conducted in the aftermath of the great democratic rituals. Still the exercise made by CPB is important. Not so much because it makes possible a better founded electoral choice: I do not think many people read a report of several hundreds of pages comparing scrupulously the economic policy proposed by various political parties, and if they did, I guess that very few people would change their vote after having read a rather tedious and fairly technical report. Still the exercise is important, because it embodies a certain idea of democracy. There is a performative dimension in this kind of projects. This is a statement against the society of appearances and its personalised lifestyle politics, a statement against the degradation of politics to a media show. It represents an intellectual input in the political process, and whatever its precise effects may be, a philosopher cannot but applaud this.

Economists are able to describe in a more detailed way the general mechanism that underscores the favourable prejudice of the philosopher. If electoral preferences are often so whimsical and so much subject to mass-psychological effects, this is because of the uncertainty that surrounds the quality of the bid made by political parties on the electoral market. According to economists, agents in electoral processes are confronted with the famous "lemon" problem. Consumers know that all second-hand cars glitter when you see them in the showroom of a dealer, but they also know that some of them are perfectly disguised wrecks (lemons). They know that some dealers on the second-hand market are crooks, and that the best crooks look particularly trustworthy. So there is asymmetric information in this kind of markets. Those who offer second-hand cars or political programmes know more about the quality of their offer than the potential purchasers. Hence the necessity of an impartial instance, an institution with a vested reputation, that is not "sold" to one of the parties and that is competent enough to distinguish what is real and what is fake, what is feasible and what is mere demagogy. If no such reliable information is provided, people are likely to quit a market where there is too much opportunity for fraud. In the realm of politics this means that antipolitical or antidemocratic reactions can be feared.

The importance of the CPB project is also closely linked to its dynamic effects. This is what I called above its "performative" dimension. The final result of the CPB calculus is far less important than the whole process through which this is achieved. The fact that political parties know that they will be subjected to the CPB scrutiny makes that they are going to devise their programmes differently. Although they know that the CPB study will not directly influence their electorate, they suppose that indirectly it does matter, because it contributes to the image of their party. Its reputation is at stake. At a moment when all political parties try by all means to catch the attention of voters and mass media, a scientific comparison of the earnest of their proposals cannot let the politicians indifferent. However, the CPB exercise may have some unexpected consequences. All programmes will be put in the same box. They will all be judged by the same standards. Proposals will have to be realistic. Generous utopias will be frowned at, unless they are considerably diluted. This will inevitably yield a homogenising effect upon these proposals. The advantage is that the formation of coalitions after the elections will be easier, at least as far as socio-economic issues are concerned. To a certain degree this is a normal consequence of the public debate. Political parties who accept the constraints imposed by such a debate will grow towards one another. The democratic debate has some civilising virtues. It implies that one is not shooting at each other from entrenched positions, but that one talks with one another. In this conversation points of view will inevitably be amended and compromises will become feasible.

However, this is not all positive. If all political parties submit to the homogenising CPB framework, then there is a chance that they will all be scrambling in the centre of the political scene, the danger being that political life as a whole will become grey, dull and predictable. Normally there is a logic in political life that prevents such a result. Opposition parties are facing other constraints than parties in government. Those who manage the state apparatus have to be able to calculate. They will try to convince the electorate with figures. And they have power. They are able to recruit a certain clientele by distributing offices and small benefits among their supporters. Meanwhile the everyday routine of management of the state threatens to evaporate the militant energies of these supporters. Hence democratic alternation and temporary passages to the opposition are important to renew political life. This gives political parties time to gather new ideas, to refresh their ideology and to address a new public. Usually people will not get mobilised by figures, but by ideas and beautiful prospects. The reply to this by the parties in government is predictable: "Your proposals are not realistic. No economist can ever take this seriously." The recent electoral debates in France between Chirac and Jospin went exactly along these lines – Chirac being a rightist president and proposing a drastic tax cut against his socialist prime minister and opponent.

If the CPB project increases pressures upon opposition parties to submit realistic proposals to the electorate, this can have as a consequence that political life loses its diversity. The agonistic element in politics, the game of rivalry and mutual defiance, will tend to vanish, especially among traditional political parties. As a consequence protest parties will pop up, rejecting all centripetal rules of the game: this is the role of extreme rightist parties in many European countries, of Pim Fortuyn's list LPF in the Netherlands. A lively democracy thus has to find a middle way. It has to civilise the various participants in the public debate, but it has also to permit a sufficient amount of diversity, rivalry and conflict in political life. Sometimes this leads to particularly hard choices for political actors. Do we admit new, radical, extremist or populist political parties to the democratic game? Do we submit them thus to its civilising virtues? Or do we have to exclude them from all this? If we choose the latter way, driven by serious indignation or by cynic calculation, aren't we offering then to these newcomers a brilliant future as outsiders defying an establishment, consisting of dull managers of the existing order?

5. POLITICAL CULTURE IN SOUTHERN AND NORTHERN EUROPE

For my country, Belgium, I would certainly advocate a similar calculus of the economic consequences of electoral programmes as CPB did in the Netherlands. As I already said, from a normative point of view it is evident that all supplementary intellectual input in the democratic process is welcome. How could a sensible person argue against a better supply of information about political options to the general public? In my country quality newspapers and magazines try already more or less successfully to fill the gap, but more and better could certainly be done. However, actual reality does not always conform to the normative schemes of ethicists and political philosophers. Seen from Belgium, there is a borderline between the political culture of the Northern and the Southern part of Europe, or between the German and the Roman world. Of course we are particularly well aware of this, because we situate our own country exactly upon this dividing line. Flemish policy makers see the Netherlands often as a kind of role model. We have copied a lot of their techniques of budget control and of public management and their system of inspection of schools and faculties. We even aim at copying their bureaucratic organisation of health care – hoping for containment of expenditures in this realm.

The CPB study is a good candidate for copying. It is neatly elaborated, solidly reasoned and well-organised; northern political culture at its best. On the other hand I expect that, whereas in the Netherlands this study will not raise fierce controversies, in Belgium and still more in France, Spain or Italy, this is totally unimaginable. Every coefficient, every hypothesis, the whole idea of such a study would be contested. The Netherlands is an orderly country. In Southern Europe political debates are much more chaotic. I remember, long ago, the debates in France about "Le Programme Commun de la Gauche", the common programme of French socialists and communists. The famous newspaper *Le Monde*, published a petition of a hundred right-wing economists against "Le Programme Commun". They proclaimed that the science of economics condemned the leftist programme with its nationalisations and its support of aggregate demand as unaffordable and economic nonsense. The Left mobilised immediately its own economists to proclaim the opposite. The debate was not uninteresting. It obliged the Left to clarify how it would finance its policy. It provoked a debate about Keynesianism, to what extent deficit spending would repay itself in the longer run, about the possibility of structural changes in the economy of a single country, about globalisation and the degree of freedom of national governments to go against the basic tendencies of the world market. Above all it made clear that economics is unable to settle a political debate. Maybe the rightist economists were more right than their opponents, but this has hardly harmed the Left. Political scandals – the diamonds Giscard d'Estaing received from an African despot – were much more determining for the issue of the elections.

In Southern Europe a rationalistic exercise like the CPB study would be looked at with a note of pity. Politicians try to speak to the heart of people, much more than to their mind. The politics of the heart prevails. Global issues are considered to be much more important than punctual ones. The distinction CPB makes between factors that can and that cannot be influenced by national policy would not be accepted. Typical of France is that the problems of globalisation are very emphatically present in recent electoral campaigns. In the Netherlands this is a rather marginal issue. Although the Dutch model is certainly interesting, rationally defensible and recommendable, it starts somewhat too much from the illusion that a well-ordered world is possible. Hence the astonishment of people in the Netherlands when chaos crops up. With the Srebrenica-affair one could still think that troubles came from the outside. The rise in 2001/02, and his murder on 6 May 2002 of Pim Fortuyn, broke down this illusion. For a long time we in the South of Europe were more aware of the fact that the world is not orderly and that it will never be in order. We would like to have some more order and rationality in our political debates. We would like to get the kind of studies CPB makes, but I guess that during the following elections in Belgium things will not be different from last time. This means: one month before the elections some journalists will remember the beautiful Dutch example of calculus of the cost of political programmes; everyone will praise the idea and subsequently conclude that there is not enough time left for organising such a calculus before the coming elections.

PART IV

ASSESSMENT OF ELECTION PROGRAMMES: CONCLUSIONS FOR THE FUTURE

CHAPTER 12

LUC VAN LIEDEKERKE

THE VIEWS OF THE POLITICAL PARTIES

1. INTRODUCTION

During the conference on calculated choices (19 April 2002), representatives of the eight Dutch incumbent political parties presented their view on the assessment effort by CPB Netherlands Bureau for Economic Policy Analysis (CPB hereafter). It is not our aim to give a full representation of the different views expressed during the conference. This is a summary exercise, presenting the outline of the argument and the main oppositions.[1] Section 2 presents the consensus among the political parties, section 3 the dissensus, and discusses the democratic quality of the calculation exercise. Section 4 concludes this contribution with some personal remarks.

2. THE CONSENSUS

Rationalistic politics

When Tinbergen launched his idea of a strong and independent central bureau for economic policy analysis, he felt that this was a necessity in a strongly ideologically segregated political landscape. The bureau was an element of rationalisation in the ideological debate, it pushed to the maximum a separation between on the one hand analytical questions, to be dealt with by able technicians (the bureau), and on the other hand the purely political choices, that provided the input for the calculation effort of the bureau. By extending the analytical component, ideological oppositions could be reduced and political dialogue facilitated. This could result in serious positive welfare effects for society at large. Implicitly, the conviction that political choices were at times foolish and short-sighted and needed a system of checks and balances to weed out the worst policy options, certainly played its part.

By and large all political parties represented in this conference, still support this rationalistic turn in politics. The possibility of separating analytical from political choices and thus the need for a (central) independent bureau for policy analysis is

Johan J. Graafland and Arie P. Ros (Eds.), Economic Assessment of Election Programmes: Does it Make Sense?, 137-144.

never put in doubt, and neither are its positive welfare effects for society. There were some concerns about precisely how far one can push the analytical part of the question and when precisely political choices should dominate, but even when discussing this issue, the argument is about the capability of economic theory to deal with issues like health care, and the underlying consensus is that if the calculation exercise could be done in a sufficiently value free way, it should be done. A rationalistic attitude in politics is for the representatives of these parties the only decent way to do politics. It is because they believe in this style of politics, that each of the parties volunteered to participate in the calculation effort.

The political parties believe in the value of CPB, in what it represents with respect to the political scene, and therefore in the value of a calculation exercise.

Welfare effects

Who benefits from the calculation exercise? Here the discussion concentrated on the question whether the main beneficiaries were the voters or rather the political parties themselves, and there seemed to emerge a consensus that in the end the direct benefits of such a calculation effort for the public at large must not be exaggerated. Few voters will read the final CPB report, but fall back upon media analysis (mostly high-profile newspapers) of the report. But press reports magnify certain results and sometimes completely forget others that might be just as interesting. At times these reports are even seriously flawed. This was nicely illustrated by the representative of the PvdA. Newspapers reported that the tax policy proposals of PvdA and GroenLinks were most favourable for high incomes, which was rather embarrassing for these parties. However, the reports misrepresented the real CPB results, because the journalists had utilised the definitions of high and low incomes used by health organisations, which do not correspond with the high/low distribution based on income profiles. Once you refer to these last definitions, the CPB calculations with respect to the tax proposals of the participating parties reflect the traditional results with leftist parties favouring low incomes, and right wing parties the opposite.

A preliminary conclusion that should be drawn from this discussion is that the beneficial effects of the exercise might increase if one succeeds in better communication of its results. This implies two things: on the one hand reaching a large public, and on the other hand guarding the quality of the information provided in the media. This theme was however not taken up in the discussion.

There was a consensus that the main beneficiaries of the exercise are the political parties themselves. The calculation effort pushes parties to be clear about their political programme and final options; it confronts them with hard choices that might be left unnoticed if not for the CPB involvement. In short: the calculation effort *disciplines* parties and precludes that wishful thinking turns into party politics. It disciplines with respect to the content of the political programme in the sense that it cannot be made up of elusive promises. It disciplines, and this might be even more important, in the sense that it pushes the discussion within the political party itself to a higher level, in which people have to think twice before introducing a proposal. Wild politics is weeded out. This has the additional advantage that cross-party discussion will become smoother, because everybody is constrained by the same analytical framework and used to the same types of ever returning arguments (what will this proposal cost, how effective can it be, *et cetera*). Political discussion civilizes through the exposure to the calculation effort. Finally, a derived advantage is that the calculation effort brings political programmes closer together and therefore simplifies the cabinet formation process.

We might even say that for a political party, participation in the calculation effort has turned into an indicator of political adulthood. This was certainly the perception of the SP, which indicated that one reason for participation in the exercise was the desire to be taken seriously by the other parties and in the end by the voters. The calculation effort is in this respect a hallmark of political respectability, and the quality of this hallmark is directly proportional to the *perceived*, and I stress this, quality of CPB itself. Fortunately, in the Netherlands CPB is widely respected. Lack of such a generally perceived high quality, political independent institute might therefore be a reason why this exercise does not take place in other countries.

3. DISSENT

What can be calculated?

The main dissent concentrated on the reach of the calculation effort. How far should we go? Calculating pure budgetary effects was considered unproblematic and necessary, but anything going beyond that was subject to discussion. Several arguments were raised:

- The results of further exercises are too uncertain to contain serious information.
- Communicating uncertain results to the public is almost impossible and leaves room for political manipulation.
- The calculation horizon (one legislative period, 4 years) is too short to find meaningful results for large institutional changes (PvdA).
- CPB is not sufficiently equipped or lacks sufficient statistical data to calculate the effects of for instance health care or education proposals. The CDA representative provided the example of a study on education which used a statistical pilot study involving only 10 pupils.
- Economics and human sciences in general are not sufficiently equipped to do the exercise.
- The exercise is too value-loaded to have any particular meaning, and results could therefore be easily politically manipulated.
- The exercise would be too costly for the taxpayer and for small political parties.

There were also arguments in favour of an extension of the calculation exercise:

- Extending the effort is a logical extension of the kind of politics we are already doing. Any additional information that helps us develop a better policy with respect to such important topics as environment, health care and transportation is helpful.

- We need a level playing field in which everybody goes through the scrutiny of the calculation effort. It is not fair that some should allow CPB to judge their health and transportation policy, and others not.
- CPB is well-positioned to know when its calculation efforts become too uncertain to be meaningful. It is certainly better positioned in this respect than the politicians themselves.
- Political parties should and can cooperate with CPB and other experts to find a common framework that allows the analysis of topics like health care, education and environment.

An interesting political divide developed with on the one hand left wing political parties like PvdA, D66, SP and GroenLinks, supporting an extension of the calculation effort, and on the other hand right wing political parties like VVD, CDA, SGP and ChristenUnie opposing it. The immediate cause for this lively discussion was that in the 2001-02 calculation exercise some parties allowed screening of their environmental and health policy, while others did not.

One institution or many?

A second topic for discussion was the question whether CPB should be the only institution doing the exercise, or whether we need to have (many) more. D66 argued that if we want to extend the calculation exercise, diversification is needed. Already in the latest calculation it was the RIVM that had to judge the environmental policy. If we want to include health care, transportation and education, we will need all the expertise available in order to reach an acceptable level of analysis. GroenLinks even proposed to subsidise universities in order to help them develop a working model capable of analysing for instance education policy in a satisfactory way. The VVD also supported a diversification of the institutions involved in order to let competitive incentives play their part.

Other parties were more reluctant to open up the horizon. The ChristenUnie for instance referred to some special features of the CPB calculation. It is the process in which a political programme is audited in an interactive way. This conversation form has educational effects for the party in itself. CPB can also rely on a considerable political status of independence that other institutes might lack. It is precisely because of this perceived independency that its judgement matters and gets media attention. Fragmented research would diminish the political status of the calculation exercise, because parties could be easily accused of shopping for the right institute with the right political colour. This would immediately wipe out the symbolic value of the entire exercise.

The special position of small political parties

The SGP, a small political party, for the first time wanted to take part in the calculation exercise of 2002. However, in the end, it decided to withdraw from the extended analysis, and clearly had mixed feelings about the calculation experience. The main problem is that the exercise demands from the political party so much input that for a small formation this is a costly investment, which some might not even be capable to afford themselves. This would certainly be the case for an extended calculation exercise. In this sense small political formations have a serious disadvantage, compared to their larger and better-funded rivals. It was clear that the present form of the calculation exercise could not eliminate this inequality.

The only thing left for small political parties would be a quick basic screening of their political programme in order to judge whether it is decent or not. This would again put a rubber-stamp on the programme, but of a far lesser quality level than the full calculation exercise. Any extension or political upgrading of the calculation effort would simply increase the political disadvantage for small parties. This cannot be the aim of CPB, who meticulously guards over the procedural fairness of the entire operation: every party should be treated in the same manner.

We are confronted here with a value dilemma: if we increase the quality and extension of the calculation effort, we will automatically disadvantage small political parties. If we want a fair procedure with no entry barriers, we will have to diminish the demands placed on the parties involved and thus the quality and meaning of the calculation effort. The representative of the SP indicated however that this argument should not be overrated, since even for his small party taking part in the calculation exercise was certainly not easy, but at the same time not impossible either.

Democratic quality of the calculation exercise

Several political representatives questioned the democratic quality of the entire exercise. There are two aspects to this. First, is it advisable that a representative of the state (CPB) controls the political parties, or should it rather be the other way round: political parties controlling CPB? Second, what is the influence of the exercise on the content of the political programme of the party? If this influence is large, we might wonder whether this is a democratic procedure for programme formation. We shall extend on both problems, taking the last one first.

The representative of the SGP reminded the audience that when you participate in the exercise, the party has to decide on many things that are usually not made explicit in the political programme. The ChristenUnie even testified that the exercise entices one into choices, which one would probably not have made after a proper consultation process.

The speed of the exercise forces party representatives to take quick, possibly even *ad hoc* decisions in order to continue the exercise. This sort of *ad hoc* decisions might extend and concretize a political programme in a highly undemocratic manner. This fear was further enhanced by a testimony of the PvdA representative responsible for the calculation exercise, who said that he decided himself on most points, with political responsibility limited to the party chairman and the party leader. It seemed impossible to all parties to consult the grassroots support during the exercise with respect to data demanded by CPB, mainly due to the speed and intensity of the calculation process, but also due to the technical quality of the exercise. GroenLinks corroborated this last point and indicated that there is quite a barrier between the insiders of the calculation exercise and the outsiders. A further extension of the exercise would probably only enhance the technocratic quality, and thus the borderline between insiders and outsiders to the process. To the extent that the calculation exercise determines the content of the political programme, this would place undue power in the hands of insiders to the exercise.

In the end, this problem rests on an empirical question: to what extent is the content of political programmes determined by the calculation exercise? The question was not explicitly debated but some remarks seemed to suggest that the impact of the exercise might in the end not be all that dramatic. According to D66, it was true that some *ad hoc* decisions had to be taken during the exercise, but the political programme presented to the voters was determined quite independently of, and well before the calculation exercise, and any adaptations afterwards could certainly not be said to touch upon the essence of the programme. This implies that although we are confronted here with a potentially big problem, reality might not be that black.

Several small parties testified that participation to the exercise could hardly be called a free choice. It is simply a question of being taken seriously or not. The SGP for instance was very reluctant to participate, but felt forced to do it because a direct political opponent (ChristenUnie) decided to join. The CPB analysis carries an aura of uprightness and truth that is hard to ignore. And once you are in the exercise, it is hard to criticize any aspect of it, precisely because you are the one who is being examined. Criticizing the master smells of bad faith and inability to cope with the results. As more political parties take part in the exercise and the extent of it increases, the political power of CPB also increases. Refusers are accused of not being capable of facing the truth, of fearing the exam because they are poorly prepared.

But is it appropriate from a democratic point of view that what is after all a governmental bureau should wield such great political power and control those who in the end have to determine the political course of a democracy? Is this not an example of Max Webers fear for bureaucratization of politics? The question is certainly valid, and if it were the case that through the exercise CPB had serious influence on party programmes, there would be ample reason for concern. But as indicated above, so far this influence seems to be rather limited. At this point the benefits of the calculation exercise (disciplining political thinking, smoothening political dialogue, *et cetera*), seem to outweigh the possible dangers. This was certainly the impression of the large political parties, who indicated that the calculation exercise, which most had gone through several times, was by now completely integrated into the functioning of the party, with neither too much influence nor too little.

4. A CHANGING POLITICAL HORIZON

At the time when CPB was launched, ideological oppositions still loomed large in society. Much of it has disappeared over the last decades. Politics, and certainly politics in the Netherlands, civilised. Dramatic political oppositions shrinked to dwarf proportions and a liberal-social democrat government shaking hands across all ideological divide became possible. CPB and the kind of politics it stands for – which is best symbolised in the idea of a calculation exercise – has certainly made a great contribution to the civilised, rationalistic approach to politics. As such CPB and its efforts for serious political dialogue are applauded by all political formations. Recently however, the political landscape has changed dramatically. New populist formations have risen spectacularly all over Europe, and though the Netherlands long seemed to escape this trend, the elections of 15 May 2002 saw a political landside that brought the apparantly unshakable home of civilised politics closer to the European mean. It is in this new political landscape that we have to think about CPB and its calculation exercise.

The disappearance of the great ideological divide was accompanied by the decline in political importance of classical interest groups like trade unions or youth movements. Traditionally, these interest groups acted like a filter on the political opinion of their members. Belonging to a trade union or a church community had a serious impact on your political convictions, but this link has now weakened and parties can no longer rely on loyal voters. Instead, they have to sell themselves directly to the voters and in this process of direct political communication the role of the media cannot be underestimated. It is often more important for a politician to take part in a talk show on TV than to formulate a parliamentary question. This disintermediation in political dialogue makes the political field highly susceptible to populist exploits. The old filter has gone, and a mediagenic character with good looks can have a sudden and tremendous impact on politics through the help of media coverage. In such a landscape one can only applaud the efforts of CPB and all political parties supporting it, to retain a serious intellectual input in the political process. If anything, the calculation effort should be further encouraged and communicated to the public in order to guarantee the quality of political conversation.

It is of course remarkable that political parties that clearly disregard the entire calculation effort not only escape public disgrace, but can even jump from nothing to the top of political ranks. How is this possible? In a certain sense the answer is that politics has become too civilised.[2] Serious opposition like the great ideological divide between socialist and conservative parties has disappeared. And although emotions can run high when politicians debate on for instance unemployment benefit regulation, it is often unclear whether the public at large notices the differences between the positions of the different parties. Politics has moved to a civilised middle position, leaving the extreme positions open.

CPB and its calculation exercise have been very successful in moving political positions closer together, too successful one might say. Rational, civilised politics has taken the heart out of political discussion, and what is left is a colourless fight that does not inspire anymore. In this open space a party with a clear and open ideology has jumped, not shying away from political incorrect positions and thereby creating real political tension. This evolution is testimony to the nature of the political process. When tensions disappears, politics dies.

Does this imply that we better stop calculating? Of course not, only it is for instance crucial that political programmes are primarily based upon political conviction rather than economic considerations.[3] The party programme formation process should come before the calculation effort. If we want to root politics with the people, we need to let political feelings speak out from the start, even if the ideas launched are highly unrealistic. The correction should come afterwards.

NOTES

1 The views expressed in this contribution are strictly personal and not official views of any of the political parties involved.

2 This argument refers to the analysis of the political process as can be found in the writings of Gilles Lipovetsky and Jean Beaudrillard.

3 It is in this respect reassuring that several political parties at the conference assured that party programmes were not written with the calculation effort in mind, but were amended later on the basis of the calculation exercise.

CHAPTER 13

JOHAN J. GRAAFLAND AND ARIE P. ROS

SUMMARY AND CONCLUSIONS

In the Netherlands, the election programmes of the political parties are assessed for their economic impact by an independent government agency, CPB Netherlands Bureau for Economic Policy Analysis (CPB). Dependent on the political setting, the CPB analysis occasionally has had a significant impact on the political scene. For example, in 1998 the analysis of CPB showed that the CDA's proposed policies would hardly foster employment. This became a fiercely debated topic and influenced the formation of the coalition after the elections. Afterwards, several economists voting for CDA doubted the quality of CPB's analysis.

The CPB analysis is a unique aspect of the Dutch elections, and is – as far as we know – not practised in other countries. The question arises whether this analysis really helps to improve the political quality of the election process and/or the quality of the economic policy proposed by the political parties. If it does, the Dutch have an innovative tool that might also be applied in other countries. If it does not, we should better stop this ritual.

The pros and cons of the CPB calculation are discussed every time the procedure is executed. This book contains contributions of several distinguished economists and philosophers who discussed this subject at the conference "Calculated choices" on 19 April 2002 in The Hague, just after the publication of the CPB analysis of the political programmes of 2002, and just before the elections in May 2002. This conference was organised by the Research Centre for Economic Policy OCFEB and the University of Tilburg. Besides economists and philosophers from various Dutch and Belgian universities, the director of CPB and the representatives of all political parties at the moment represented in parliament participated in this conference. The questions discussed in the various papers are both political and economic. Political questions, for example, are:

- Does the CPB analysis improve the democratic quality of the elections?

Johan J. Graafland and Arie P. Ros (Eds.), Economic Assessment of Election Programmes: Does it Make Sense?, 145-151.

- Does the strong focus on the economic effects of the political programmes induce the neglect of other relevant aspects of the programmes, including non-economic aspects and economic aspects which are difficult to quantify?
- Does CPB analysis impact the choices of the voters?
- How much attention should CPB pay to the programmes of large and small political parties? Do all parties have the right on an equal share of the CPB expertise?

In addition, several contributors were asked to consider the quality of the CPB analysis from a scientific economic perspective. In particular, the following questions were put forward:
- What is the scientific status of the instruments used by CPB to analyse the consequences of the electoral programmes?
- Can we really be so confident of the tools of economic science that we allow CPB's report to have a major impact on the elections and the formation of the coalition for the next four years?
- How can we find a balance between using the information provided by economics without disregarding the uncertainty involved with this type of analysis? What does a proper balance imply for the presentation of the results?
- How transparent is the procedure applied by CPB?
- Do we need more economic institutes to analyse the economic consequences of the political programs?

Table 1 presents an overview of the political advantages and disadvantages of the economic analysis of the electoral programmes mentioned by the various contributors. In this concluding chapter, we refrain from repeating all these arguments. Rather, we would like to note that the main advantages (on which most contributors agree) are intrinsically connected to some disadvantages. For example, whereas the CPB analysis is a disciplining device that stimulates parties to be more realistic and requires more exact formulations, this aspect also creates a tendency towards technocratic policy making and a loss of political diversity. Similarly, where the CPB analysis increases the intellectual input and fosters the trust and openness for discussion, it also reduces the room for more specific political ideals and visions, including alternative visions of political parties on the economy. A third intrinsic tension is that the analysis offered by the CPB principally increases the quality of policy programmes, but at the same time works as a filter that hampers innovative policy proposals.

Table 1 Overview of political advantages and disadvantages of the CPB analysis[a]

Political advantages	*Political disadvantages*	*Who benefits?*
Provides information to the parties and voters (7,8,12)	Hampers innovative policy proposals (1,4,7,9)	Politicians get better insight in economic consequences of their proposals (1,3,6,12)
Disciplining device: makes party programmes more realistic and consistent (1,3,4,6,7,9,10,12)	Tendency towards technocratic and pragmatic policy making with focus on economic arguments and less room for specific political visions and meanings of the common good (1,10,12)	Politicians can convince the public of economic soundness of their programmes (7,10,12)
Requires more exact formulations of proposals and clarifies the programmes, leaving no room for demagogy or manipulation (1,3,4,6,7,8,9,10)	Lack of democratic base of detailed input of analysis (1,3,12)	CPB analysis is a plaything for political parties in the struggle for power (10)
Level playing field, focus on political choices rather than economic arguments (1,3,4,12)	Selected use of outcomes by political parties and selected presentation in the media (4)	Voters are not directly served by the CPB analysis because of its complexity, but they pay the costs (taxes) (1,4,7,10,11,12)
Makes coalition formation easier (1,3,4,7,9,10,11,12)	Political parties in government have more information (6)	Voters benefit from better programme design and faster cabinet formation process (7,8)
Improved access to information for political parties not in government (6)	Principled parties have more difficulty with quantification of their priorities (10)	CPB can test its models on serious and also eccentric proposals (1)
Willingness to submit programmes to CPB creates atmosphere of trust, openness and readiness for discussion (7,10,11,12)	Commitment to exact proposals is weak, because of need of coalition formation afterwards. Political parties need room for negotiation (10)	
Analysis prevents degradation to politics as media show by raising the intellectual input (11)	Loss of political diversity, especially among traditional political parties (11)	
	Analysis does not evaluate in terms of specific objectives of political parties and the internal consistency of the programmes. The voter is implicitly addressed as a floating voter (10)	

Table 1 Overview of political advantages and disadvantages of the CPB analysis[a]

Political advantages	*Political disadvantages*	*Who benefits?*
	The analysis is too costly for small parties (12)	
	Political parties cannot criticize CPB and political power of CPB increases; the room for party opinions on economics decreases (12)	
	Political parties have no free choice to participate in CPB analysis (12)	

[a] The authors expressing these opinions are indicated by their chapter numbers. The numbers correspond to, respectively:

1. Keuzenkamp	6. Graafland	10. Van Erp
3. Don	7. Van der Lecq	11. Vandevelde
4. Den Butter	8. Swank	12. Political parties (see Van Liedekerke)
5. Jacobs, Kuper and Sterken	9. Bomhoff and Van der Geest	

A fourth type of paradox is that the CPB analysis on the one hand fosters equal opportunities of political parties, but, as the analysis becomes more and more extended, on the other hand it tends to favour large political parties and parties in government (who have more access to information present in the ministries), whereas the democratic legitimation and political commitment to the detailed proposals required as input for these analysis decreases. A final political tension is that, although most political parties say that they voluntarily participate in the CPB analysis, there is no real free choice anymore. Hence, although CPB intends to serve the political parties, at the same time it restricts the political freedom of these parties. As stated by Vandevelde, a lively democracy has to find a middle way between the civilization and rationalisation of the public debate and the amount of diversity, rivalry and conflict in political life. Finally, we suspect that these tensions and the disadvantages which are intrinsic to the CPB analysis of the electoral programmes may increase if the analysis is extended to even more aspects of the political agenda, as some of the political parties proposed (see the debate in Van Liedekerke). If the traditional political parties allow CPB to replace the variety in ideas about the effects of even more policy proposals by a CPB judgement, the technocratic and bureaucratic character of the election process may become so high that the benefits for the political parties (more insight and certification of financial soundness of their program) may fall short of the disadvantage of an increasing reluctance of voters to commit themselves to highly homogeneous political parties.

This may especially be true if the CPB analysis pretends too much certainty and if the CPB instruments are insufficient to capture the complex reality. Although CPB has a good reputation in policy and academic circles, both with respect to the quality of its analysis and instruments, as well as with respect to its integrity and independency, still there is a lot of criticism on the quality of the CPB study as shown by Table 2. Again there are some intrinsic tensions, which will not be easily

Table 2 Overview of positive and negative economic criticism on CPB analysis and the use of involving more institutes[a]

Positive qualities of CPB analysis and instruments	*Criticism on CPB analysis and instruments*		*Advantages of more institutes*	*Disadvantages of more institutes*
High quality of CPB analysis regarding budgetary and income effects (1,6)	Models not suitable for drastic structural changes (1,7,9)	CPB lacks sufficient data to evaluate the effects of *e.g.* health care or education proposals (12)	Would give more insight in uncertainty of analysis (3,6)	Too much investments required (1,3,4)
CPB models are state-of-the-art instruments (5)	False pretences, CPB presents no sensitivity analysis whereas figures are subject to uncertainty (1,3,5,6,7,12)	Impossible to exclude normative and subjective interpretations of CPB (4,6,7,12)	Assessment not locked in CPB framework and will raise the quality of evaluation (3,7,9)	Loss in clarity, comparability and consistency of results, communication of results becomes more difficult (1,3,6,12)
Integrity and independency of CPB (6,12)	Analysis does not deal with the many effects for which many proposals are designed (like health care, education, safety, traffic, quality of public services) (3,4,9)	Uncertainty about dynamics of economic effects (4,6)	More competition leads to more lively political debate (9)	Danger of selective use (3,12)
Well-organised process of the analysis (6,12)	Some room for misrepresentation of economic effects of election programmes (3,12)	Results are not reproducible by outsiders (4,5,6)		More difficult to keep information confidential (6)
CPB has good access to information because of its numerous contacts with policy makers (4)	No presentation of long-term effects (3,7,12)	Danger of lock-in CPB framework (4,6,7)		
	CPB instruments are very complex, no use of smaller scale systems (5)	CPB instruments are not fully consistent (4,6)		
	No forward-looking behaviour and dynamic budget constraint in models (5)	No insight in strengths and weaknesses of Dutch economy compared to other countries (9)		

a See table 1.

solved in the future. Whereas the analysis does not deal with many potentially relevant effects of the proposals (including long-term effects, dynamic constraints and non-economic effects), extending the analysis in this way would further complicate the study and endanger its consistency. Moreover, as the uncertainty of these effects will tend to be even larger, the false pretence of certainty implicit in the point estimates of CPB may further increase. Also the role of normative and subjective interpretations of CPB and the problem of a lack of transparency and reproducibility will tend to increase if more issues are covered by the CPB analysis. Performing sensitivity analysis on the effects of all policy proposals for which strong empirical evidence is lacking will, however, makes it progressively difficult to communicate the results and, in the end, completely takes away the informative value of the CPB study. Also the room for misrepresentation of the results by political parties will increase with the complexity and volume of the study.

Similar tensions are present when the CPB study is supplemented by economic analyses of competing economic institutes. Although alternative studies would allow a more intersubjective judgement and give more insight in the uncertainty involved with the quantitative estimates, it will also reduce the clarity and consistency and make the communication of the results more difficult. Also the danger of selective use will be higher, whereas it is yet unclear which institute has both the ability and the reputation to fulfil this task.

A more fruitful approach might be the proposal of Den Butter (see Table 3), who proposes, on the one hand, to ask second opinions from other institutes on those parts of the programmes for which CPB is highly qualified and that, on the other hand, other institutes are asked for issues that require other types of analyses in the field of their competences. Also some political parties argue that other experts like universities should be involved and they are prepared to subsidize this kind of activities. Den Butter also proposes a supervisory committee of independent technical experts which could be helpful in explaining the crucial assumptions in the exercise, thereby raising the transparency of the study. The uncertainty of the CPB analysis could also be made more visible by a (limited set of) sensitivity analyses, as proposed by Den Butter, Graafland and Sterken *et al.* Moreover, Graafland and Sterken *et al.* also plea for the additional use of small models that illustrate the main mechanisms which would also increase the transparency of the analysis.

Finally, there are some proposals for performing some different types of analysis. For example, Den Butter argues for a post mortem analysis of previous assessments of the election programmes, which could help to place the relative importance of policy programmes in historical perspective. Bomhoff and Van der Geest plea for an international study of the strengths and weaknesses of the Dutch economy in comparison with other countries. This will provide background information to the political parties that will help them to identify relevant policy measures. For both studies it holds that they can be disconnected from the election time. The proposal of Van Erp to disconnect the elections and the CPB analysis, however, seems to be a step too far in the direction of nullifying the political relevance of it. After all, notwithstanding the numerous shortcomings and disadvantages involved with this study, all participants, including the representatives of the political parties, believe that the net value of a (limited) study is positive. The question is rather how far the CPB analysis should be extended beyond the presentation of the budgetary and income effects of the political programmes.

Table 3 Overview of proposals [a]

More interaction with academics, ask second opinions from other institutes (1,4)
Subsidize other institutes (universities) to stimulate diversification (12)
Qualitative analysis by other experts of proposals that cannot be implemented in models (4,7)
Introduce a supervisory committee of independent experts (4)
Sensitivity analysis with some crucial assumptions or density forecast to represent uncertainty (4,5,6,7)
Use of a small model that highlights main mechanisms and improve transparency (5,6)
Models and complete databank on the web (1)
International comparison of strengths and weaknesses of the Dutch economy (9)
Post mortem analysis of plans and outcomes (4)
Disconnect CPB analysis from elections (10)

a See table 1.

INDEX